Investing to Achieve Your Life's Desires

A manual for professionals, managers and other busy people having little time to follow their investments

The secret to investing wisely, while living your busy life

Robert H. Scott, Jr.

All Rights Reserved, Copyright 2013

Foreword

This book was originally written in 1991 and was entitled "Investing for the 1990's and beyond." Events since that time have changed the investment landscape and make a new edition necessary for those investing in the 21st Century.

What are my credentials to write this book? I graduated Magna Cum Laude with high honors in economics from Kenyon College where I was a member of Phi Beta Kappa. I graduated from Duke University Law School with honors, law review, Order of the Coif honorary fraternity. After four years of service in the Air Force with one year in the Vietnam theater with Special Operations I returned to Kansas City with the largest tax law firm in Kansas City from which I was recruited two years later to become counsel to then Federated Department Stores (now Macy's) rising to Operating Vice President and Senior Counsel (2nd to General Counsel) in my eleven years with them. I left to take the place of a friend appointed Federal Judge with me taking his place in his law firm. I later left the firm to pursue charitable and business interests which continue to this day. From the time I was 13 I have owned stocks and have been a successful investor for nearly 50 years. Am I Warren Buffett? No, not even close! But I had a busy career with little time to handle my investments and I needed a strategy that let me profit from my investments while not adversely affecting my career. I suspect many of you may be in the same situation. Over the years that strategy has evolved into the one I currently employ. It is this strategy that I have shared with my family and now hope to share with a larger readership who I hope will also benefit.

As of the date of this writing (2013) I have a compounded annual 2% positive after inflation and after tax return over the 30 year period 1982-2013. While that does not sound like a great return consider that it works out to around a 10% compounded annual pre inflation, pre tax return. One focus of this book will be the emphasis on after inflation and after tax returns. You will see shortly I am going to suggest you target trying to achieve a 25% annual return before inflation and taxes. Very difficult to achieve but not entire impossible and the closer you come to that return the better off you will be. Had I not reached for a 25% return I suspect that my results would be far worse. There were a number of personal reasons that I held significant cash during some of these periods that adversely affected my overall return and you may find you are in a similar situation. So while I strive for 25% I am happy to have achieved 10% annual returns although I hope you can do much better….and are a bit luckier! Reality is you will likely achieve a 10-15% return but only if you strive for better.

All the usual caveats apply here. Past performance is no guarantee of future performance. Thoughts in this book are merely ideas I am sharing and in no way should be considered investment advice. There are plenty of sources of investment advice and you should take advantage of those in making your own investment plan. Nothing in this book is to be considered either legal or tax advice. For specific investment, legal and tax advice you need to consult your own advisors. But hopefully this book will help you to have meaningful discussions with those you choose to provide you advice.

Many of the rules and concepts in the earlier book are still applicable, but with development of the internet, globalization and a vast new array of new investment products to be successful with your investments today requires a new look and some new planning. The purpose of this book is to keep the tried and true rules while building on those to understand how the new investment world can be made to work for you.

Most of those who have money to invest also are very busy people. Managing a career, having relationships, raising a family and just dealing with all the day to day details of life in the 21st Century is a major undertaking. At the same time investing wisely for the future can at times be overwhelming. While some people thrive on managing their investments most would rather just have their investments working for them to achieve their goals, be that early retirement, funds for children's college, starting their own business or one of many other goals for which they are saving and investing. This book tries to simplify the process and hopefully help you take away some of the stress that investments can bring.

To prepare an investment book that is useful to those with little knowledge of investments, those with a basic knowledge and those who have considerable expertise is difficult. Making it too simple or too complex can render it useless. Each of us has certain ideas about what we want our investments to accomplish for us in our lifetime. They may be rather vague (like," I want to retire someday") or far more detailed "(I want to retire in Italy with a vineyard in my early fifties"). So what works for one person with one objective (saving for retirement at an early age) may not work for another person whose objective may be to own their own business and be their own boss after years of working for larger organizations. As life teaches us, all things change. Where we thought we would be in our lives 20 years ago often differs from where we end up 20 years later. And the ups and downs of the financial world have left many an investment plan in shambles, if not worse, just as you had planned to make use of your financial resources.

What this book hopes to achieve is to help you to identify what you are investing for, what are the realistic goals you can achieve and then to help you balance busy and active lives and careers with an investment plan that is easy to manage and yet will put you on a firm financial footing for your future….whatever future you have chosen.

The techniques in this book helped me to retire at an early age, help my children through college and graduate schools and into their careers without a burden of debt and despite the loss of my wife of 45 years to cancer to continue on with my life without a change in living standards. Easy sounding goals; not so easy to actually achieve.

This is not a book about getting rich, or staying rich if you already have achieved that, but is a book about spreading your risks, identifying and balancing your goals and developing techniques that will let you live your lives without devoting excessive parts of that life to managing investments.

The Latin phrase from Horace, *Carpe diem, quam minimum credula postero,* can be translated as "Seize the day, put no trust in tomorrow." While some view this as a recommendation to live only for today it seems to me more a warning not to put excessive reliance on what tomorrow may bring therefore living for tomorrow instead of enjoying the pleasures of today. But to ignore the future entirely may make tomorrow far less pleasurable than today. It is the balance between living day to day and yet giving the future its due that we seek to achieve. I wrote about this in my second book, "I Love You...I Love You More!" written after my wife's death and trying to draw lessons from our very successful, if far too short, 45 years of marriage.

In my first book, "How To Keep What You Make," I describe a way for handling your money to lessen the stress that comes from having discretion on how to spend that income. It is easy to handle finances when you have so little that you do not have choices. Most of us in high school or college remember those days. Allowances or earnings we made in that time went for clearly identified expenses. But as you start to work you accumulate more and more income and it is far less easy to manage successfully. Often poor money management can lead to financial troubles or worse. This book takes money management one step further, looking at how you handle the build up of what is not needed for day to day living and how to have your savings and investments work to make your life easier and happier. Without spending excessive time doing so. Time better spent on your careers, family and just living life.

While living busy lives and building a career having time to consider what to do with savings and investments is no easy task. Often it is ignored entirely or turned over to someone we think is a professional at handling investments. As many a celebrity has found (or those investing with Bernie Maddoff or others of his ilk) this is not always a formula for success. Finding an honest and capable investment advisor can be a major challenge and for those with smaller amounts to invest it can be nearly impossible. It is hoped this book will help you through the process and result in developing your own plan that will give you true investment success while not monopolizing your time or having you abdicate responsibility to someone you can only hope will have your best interests at heart.

A word of warning. This book tries to cover a large range of material before getting into how to use it in a simple and easy manner to develop a diversified portfolio and mange it without driving yourself crazy.

Much of this material you will read one time just to have the background you need to prepare yourself for putting together a solid plan that will not require your day to day management.

So why cover areas you will only look at once? Because much of the material covers items that you will come across or which will be promoted to you by advisers, friends or family. In many ways it is like having a vaccination against illness, only in this case financial illness. So when the book discusses timing strategies, fundamental analysis, etc. understand this is to prepare you for making good decisions as you manage your financial assets for whatever goals you have for yourself be it retirement, opening your own business, or all the other possibilities ahead of you.

For those who may find they cannot wait for the recommendations later in this book here is a short version-

A simple and less involved program of investment is discussed first, for those wanting a simple system of investing instead of the more detailed program discussed in this book and outlined below.

If this fits your needs then the following is something for you to consider. I still recommend you read this book in its entirely but in the end you may find this meets your investment needs.

The program suggested is one that was included in a recent weekly newsletter (October 31, 2013) from the American Association of Individual Investors (AAII). It includes use of 5 Vanguard Mutual Funds allocating 20% to each and rebalancing twice a year (May 1 and November 1) but only if a fund is under 15% or over 25% at the time you rebalance.

If these funds are held in an account to which you add funds you would add 20% in each of these funds each time you add money to your account for investment no matter the percentage they represent at that time unless it is one of the two dates for rebalancing.

You will not hit a home run with this program but it is simple and easy for someone who is too busy to manage their investments actively or just does not want to spend the time or effort to be more deeply involved in their investments.

This investment program may be used for either taxable or nontaxable accounts.

If you are in a 401(k) plan that does not include these Vanguard funds then choose funds that are as close in resemblance to these funds. And if you ultimately roll that account into an IRA you can then use these funds in the rollover IRA account.

If you use a broker it is likely that these Vanguard funds are available on a no commission basis. If not you can go to Vanguard directly.

This program differs from the one in this book but I realize that many of you want something very, very simple.

The 5 Vanguard funds are:

1. Vanguard SP500 Index Fund (VFINX)
2. Vanguard Small Cap Value Fund (VISVX)
3. Vanguard REIT Index Fund (VGSIX)
4. Vanguard All World ex US Index Fund (VFSVX)
5. Vanguard Intermediate Term, Investment Grade Bond Fund (VFICX)

Some of the advice that follows will still apply, such as maximizing use of Roth IRA and 401(k) Plans. But for each of your investment accounts this allocation is one for you to consider with those providing you investment advice.

Can see how this has performed over the years in the following chart that was prepared off of Yahoo Finance November 9, 2013 using following link:
http://finance.yahoo.com/q/bc?s=VFINX&t=my&l=on&z=l&q=l&c=visvx%2Cvgsix%2Cvfsvx%2Cvficx

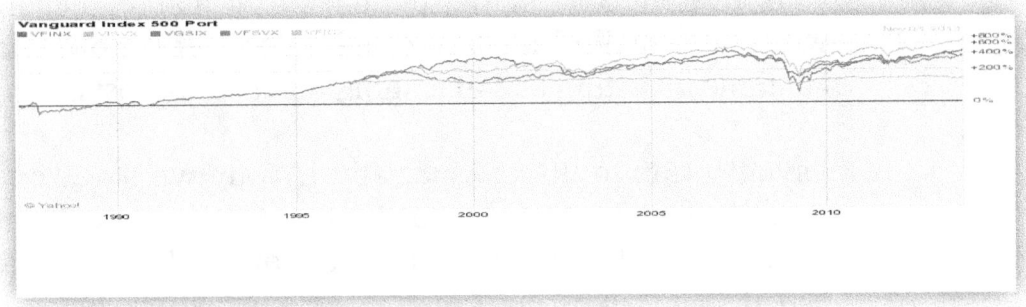

For those who want a more active involvement with their investments with a chance of doing better than average returns the following will be recommended.

1. Make maximum use of Roth, Traditional IRA and 401K or other tax free or tax favored plans. If employer matches be especially sure to contribute enough to get maximum matching. But do not fill these with your employer's stock as many did to their regret at Enron!

2. Diversify among no fewer than five and no more than ten mutual funds. If in a personal account (vs. 401(k) for example) use no load funds with low expenses such as Vanguard or Fidelity. And no, I have no relationship with either firm other than as a customer.

3. If using discount broker for personal accounts be sure you know if there are inactivity fees, maintenance fees and the cost of trading. Most firms today have no cost purchase and sale of no load mutual funds, but beware of early out fees. These are investment vehicles not trading vehicles.

4. Spread your investments over a variety of categories e.g., large cap, mid cap and small cap funds as well as some international funds. If you are young then emphasize more the small cap funds but never more than 25% in any one category.

5. Use added contributions to 401(k) and other funds to average your overall cost in those funds. A market decline while wrenching may ultimately prove to be very profitable as you continue investing and averaging down your costs.

6. Pay attention to taxes, especially if you own stock or funds in taxable accounts but do not let taxes drive your investments. Lock in any losses (watching out for wash sale) before year end if that makes tax sense in your situation and if older be aware of the step up in basis on death of your assets you may wish to leave your children (assuming the law does not change).

7. Check and reallocate your investments twice a year. I use May 8 and October 8 but May 1 and November 1 have strong statistical reasons for that choice. I use October 8 because other than 1929 and 1987 I have found that by November 1 the markets have usually run up from October 8.

8. Consider using a 75%/25% rule in investing when investing and when reallocating. I generally am 75% invested in the stock market and 25% in cash or cash-like assets. Reason is that when I reallocate if I have 85% stocks I will take 10% and move to a cash type asset or if I have fallen to 65% I would add 10% to stocks from cash with appropriate allocations within my portfolio. Why? Because this causes me to take some profits in up markets (hopefully in tax advantaged accounts such as IRA or 401(k)) or if markets have declined to reinvest up to my allocation. Why maintain 75% in stocks if convinced the market will go down? Because it is very, very hard to time markets accurately. And if you are wrong you will likely end up with subpar performance. Better to go through the valley of a downturn than to miss the upturn you did not see coming. Keeping 25% in cash type assets will adversely affect your performance but it gives you funds to buy on a dip and makes a decline a bit less painful. Studies show we hate losses more than we like gains….like two and a half times as much! So this cushion of cash takes away some of the pain that will come from inevitable downs in markets.

But doing this takes discipline! Your brain will want to talk you out of sticking to your plan but you need to stiffen yourself to holding to your plan. Sounds easy but believe me in fifty years of investing I have found this far from easy. There is no magic in 75/25 and depending on your circumstances and tolerance for market swings you may consider 80/20 or even 90/10. But whatever you pick as right for you stick with it and change it only if circumstances change. For example if in your 40's and otherwise in good shape financially you might consider 90/10 moving to 80/20 in your 50's and then 75/25 in your 60's. In your 70's you might even go to 70/30%.

9. Between times of allocation try not to focus on the roller coaster of the markets. It can drive you crazy or worse cause you to make crazy decisions. Stocks are one of the few things that people tend to buy when they are expensive and sell when they are cheap.

10. Consider a few (but no more than 5% of your portfolio) in high risk/high return small capitalization stocks. These are stocks that if they succeed will reward you with 10 to 100 times or more your investment. They are also stocks that can go bust and lose your entire investment. I have had both happen. Spreading these among ten small capitalization stocks gives you a great chance to increase your overall performance. You will be surprised what one home run stock will do to your average performance.

11. Remember always that you are investing not trading and that this is something you will be doing all through your life. The objective is to end up ahead of taxes and inflation and hopefully substantially ahead.

Later in this book all of this will be discussed in more detail but as the first part of the book is devoted to overview I feel important to give you a brief synopsis of what will be discussed later about how to set up your own investments to hopefully take advantage of what the stock market can do to make your life better.

Table of Contents

Foreword	2
Preface	10
Overview	18
Introduction	19
Chapter 1. Accumulating and Holding Wealth	27

    1.1 Introduction
    1.2 Education
    1.3 Careers and Business
    1.4 Investments in General
    1.5 Investment Choices
    1.6 Real Estate
    1.7 Collectibles
    1.8 Gold, Treasury Bills and other "Safe" Investments
    1.9 Common Stocks
    1.10 Options, Convertibles, Preferred Stocks, Etc.
    1.11 Conclusion

Chapter 2. Stock Market 101 – Efficient Market vs. ?	42
Chapter 3. Stock Market 201 – Gurus	47

    3.1 In General
    3.2 Newsletters
    3.3 Fundamental
    3.4 Technical
    3.5 Astrological
    3.6 Hulbert
    3.7 Electronic Gurus, CNBC, PBS, FOX, BLOOMBERG, CNN.
    3.8 Super Bowl Indicator

Chapter 4. Stock Market 301 – Market Timing	62

    4.1 Buy and Hold
    4.2 Timing Strategies
    4.3 Stop Loss Strategy
    4.4 Market Cycles

Chapter 5. Economic Background beyond 2010	83

    5.1 Demographic and Scientific Developments

    5.2 War and Peace

Chapter 6. Some Uncommon Thoughts About Investing   90

    6.1 Allocations: Cash, Bonds and Stocks
    6.2 After Tax Reform: Forget Individual Stocks?
    6.3 IRA and Other Tax Deferred Investing
    6.4 More on Taxes
    6.5 Look for Strategies
    6.6 Brokers – Pay for What you Get

Chapter 7. Design of Your Personal Investment Program   108

    7.1 Cash Reservoir for Down Years
    7.2 Investment Fund – How and Where to Hold
    7.3 Your Investment Funds – What to Hold and How toBuy

Chapter 8. Making The Program Work   126

    8.1 Emotions and Investing
    8.2 Keep an Eye on Market Basics
    8.3 Stay With Your Plan!
    8.4 Changing Conditions

Chapter 9. Keeping Score   134

    9.1 Performance Charting
    9.2 Other ways of Keeping Track

Chapter 10. Concluding Thoughts   141

    10.1 Count on Change
    10.2 Seeding, Weeding and Succeeding
    10.3 Never Eat Your Seed Corn

Resources and Links   144

Your Personal Investment Plan   146

Preface

This book aims at helping the investor target a 25% annual investment return – before taxes and before inflation. Opps, don't close the book thinking this guy is nuts! If 25% annual return sounds out of reach consider the following which explains why such a high return objective is necessary. Despite the market meltdowns of 1987, 2000 and 2008-9 (not to mention 1929) viewed over the long term I believe such a target is worth setting as a target goal. Will you achieve it, probably not. I am not saying it is easy and certainly not that you can expect a 25% return year after year. There will be times your portfolio will decline by half or even more no matter how well diversified you might be. But following the ideas in this book you will not view those as disasters but as opportunities. And no, you may not make this objective and in fact you probably won't, but the closer you can come to it the better off you will be. I am not going to pretend I have achieved this target because I have not. But in my tax free accounts I have achieved a positive return after allowing for inflation and taxes. And believe me, that is no mean feat. And I started serious investing with my own money at a terrible time, 1966. I had been an investor since the early 1950's but not with serious money. Then in 1971 I inherited a good deal of money only to get hit with the major downturn of the early 1970's. And in 1987 I actually would have turned out ok but my broker entered a buy order for a major position instead of a sell order on the Friday before Black Monday with its over 20% drop. It was the daughter of a friend who made the error and there was no way to correct it. I decided to do the right thing and with the help of my friend ultimately worked my way out of the hole. Fortunately I had raised significant amounts of cash going into the crash that let me cover the purchase. But it did not help my overall return! To say the least. And in 2008 I had two large CD's come due just in time for Ameriprise to put them into the Reserve Fund which was promptly frozen. As a result I had that money tied up for nearly two years. Despite all of this I have come out ahead in 30 years in IRA investing after taking inflation into account and calculating a 25% estimated tax rate.

For comparison, the S&P 500, a good price weighted index to compare your performance against, peaked in 1971 at 1000 and declined to 500 two years later. Because of inflation this was in reality a much worse decline than 50%. In fact it came close to the overall decline after the 1929 crash (that decline actually occurred in the early 1930's as the market recovered quickly after the 1929 crash only to turn down sharply into its ultimate 90% decline). What would the S&P 500 need to be today to compare to 1971 dollars? 5775 and as of September 19, 2013 the index was only at 1772. As this was a time when I had a large inheritance from my grandparents come to me I have compared where I was then to where I am now and my total portfolio has in fact outperformed the S&P after deducting for inflation and even after deducting for taxes despite long periods where I held cash for a variety of personal reasons. Have I achieved 25% annual compounded returns? Hardly! Don't I wish. But I do know had I not tried for higher returns I likely would not have been successful in beating the S&P 500 after inflation and after taxes for over 40 years. Had I actually achieved a 25% per year compounded return fully invested during that period I would now be a billionaire! Alas, not even close! Instead my rate has been closer to 6% per annum compounded. But of course during this time I held cash, owned homes, educated a family and incurred all those other expenses we all encounter through life. To me those are the real returns from investing.

So don't think you will likely achieve 25% annual compounded returns. I use those as a target for reasons you will see coming up very shortly.

Later in this book I will set out a suggested investment program for people who are too busy to spend much time planning and watching their investments. But before we get to that plan it is important to understand some fundamentals of investing. Fundamentals that will make the difference between being a success or a failure in your investment plan. You will only need to learn the fundamentals once and thereafter you can focus on your plan and making it work for you with the least amount of attention. You will still have to do some work on your investments but this book is intended to help you spend as little time as necessary to get the most out of your funds for investment.

Most of this book you will read only one time and then you can focus on the techniques I suggest you consider to make investing profitable with the least amount of your time and focus. Leaving you to lead your busy lives without having to spend an inordinate amount of time with your investments. So do not get discouraged when this book discusses many fundamentals since these you will only have to consider once as a background for the investment program covered later in the book.

For those of you who are not familiar with financial calculators do not let the discussion below scare you. The results are what are important and you do not have to be a math whiz or calculator wizard to understand the end result. But for those who do understand how to use these tools the methodology is included.

Now let us turn to an important example which illustrates the importance of fixing appropriate goals for your investments.

A 50 year old executive, Fred, takes early retirement. He is given a severance package which includes $100,000 in his profit sharing account that can be rolled over into an IRA (Individual Retirement Account).

Considering his options, Fred looks at investing for a 10%, a 15%, a 20% and a 25% annual return. He plans to leave this money in the IRA, without touching it, until Fred is 65. Then he plans to withdraw it over the next 20 years.

The following table shows just what a whopping difference a few percentage points in annual return can mean for Fred!

$100,000 increased for 15 years, then withdrawn over 20 years, results in the following annual income, after deducting 5% a year for inflation:

At %	ANNUAL INCOME BEFORE TAX BUT AFTER INFLATION	ANNUAL INCOME MINUS 50% TAX
25%	$268,734	$134,367
20%	113,835	56,917
15%	44,454	22,227
10%	15,792	7,896

Notice the difference for Fred between a 10% annual return and even a 15% return. If he can achieve a 20 or 25% return his income in his golden years will truly be golden!

This same example applies as well to a younger person setting aside $2,000 a year in an IRA. For example, a 36 year old putting aside $2,000 a year in an IRA and earning 25% a year compounded would have $110,101 by the time they reach Fred's age of 50. That is $110,101 in what those dollars were worth when they were 36 and started their process.

To arrive at these figures you need a financial calculator. One that allows you to calculate future values and present values. To simplify the task for you the table below gives you the percentages you will need to easily "deflate" future dollars, assuming a 5% average annual inflation rate for the annual percentages shown. This assumes that no tax is currently payable on these amounts, as in the case of an IRA, 401(k) or other tax advantaged vehicle. As an aside, at the time this book is written in 2013 inflation is running less than 5% using government figures but there is a risk of much higher inflation down the road. For our purposes 5% is a longer term average in the post WWII era. As with most things in investing, inflation and taxes are both moving targets.

DEFLATION TABLE FOR FUTURE VALUES

Annual % Increase	To Deflate Use this % Increase
25%	19.05%
20%	14.29%
15%	9.52%
10%	4.76%

An example, using this table may help. First we will do some calculations without using the table.

Take Fred's case again. He wants to know how much his $100,000 will be worth in 15 years, when he is 65. Using his financial calculator he enters 15 in "n" (number of years), he then enters 25 in the "I" (for annual interest), and finally he enters 100,000 in "PV" (for present value). He pushes the button marked "FV" to get the future value of his $100,000 in 15 years at 25%. The answer is $2,842,170.

To "deflate" this total; that is to see what those dollars at age 65 are worth in today's dollars, when Fred is 50, he enters the following in his financial calculator: 15 in "n" then 5 in "I" (for 5% a year inflation) and in FV (future value) he puts in the FV calculated above of $2,842,170 after which he pushes PV (for present value) and he arrives at a current, or present, values of $1,367,132. This means that is $2.8 million in the future will only buy in current dollars $1.3 million in goods and services.

Using the table above Fred can more easily find the same answer. He starts by entering 15 in "n", then enters 19.05 (the deflated percentage equal to 25% including inflation) in "I." He then puts his $100,000 in PV and pushes the FV button. The result? $1,367,543. Roughly the same result he found in the longer method but with a lot less trouble.

Fred isn't done yet. He now wants to know what amount he can take out of this fund if it keeps growing at 25% a year for the next 20 years, after he is 65. He wants to know in current (age 50 dollars) what those dollars are worth to him.

To do this Fred enters 20 in the "n" for the 20 year period he is considering. Then he enters from our table 19.05 in "I" which is the deflated value of 25% a year. Finally he enters the deflated result from his previous calculations, $1,367,543 in PV. He pushes the PMT button ("PMT" stands for payments) and the result is $268,734.

If you look back at the first table you will see that $268,734 is the before tax annual amount that Fred will have from his investments if he earns 25% a year on these investments. This how we arrived at that amount in the table.

I hope that this powerful example is enough to convince you that shooting for a 20 or 25% investment return is worth it. If you think so, then read this book and find out how you might achieve these results in your own investment program. No one can guarantee any result in the future much less one with this very large return. Your results may be far less than this but it makes a sensible target for you to consider.

Overview

This is a book by a private investor for private investors. It was written originally only for use by my family. My idea was to develop an investment manual that passed on to them what investment wisdom I have accumulated in over 50 years investing.

During the time I have been investing I have made some dandy mistakes! But, I have also enjoyed considerable success as well. Enough so that I hoped my family would find some of what I have learned to be of help in the handling of their money. It would give me great satisfaction to know that they can enjoy the unique freedom that comes from having independent means, if only they will work to achieve it.

If this book is also of help to other private investors who are seeing to manage money wisely, then the effort will be doubly rewarding.

As will become evident, it is not an easy task to manage money well. Harder than most people realize. But that does not mean it has to be an all consuming task. The best discussion of how difficult it is to just preserve capital is a 1988 article in Forbes Magazine entitled "Preserving the Family Fortune." This article is important enough that I hope you can find a copy of it. In order to avoid copyright issues I am not including it here unfortunately. But if you can find a copy then reading it may help to understand why I have adopted the investment methods discussed in the rest of this book.

Introduction

The greatest risk to American fortunes is taxation. If you found and have read the Forbes article, you may challenge me saying "I thought he said that inflation was the biggest risk!" You are correct, but I ask you to consider whether inflation is not really just another form of taxation, carefully and deceptively hidden, but nevertheless taxation.

Before discussing this a word of warning about this book. Often I will go into subjects in a depth that the average manager or professional will find beyond them. I do this so you will understand the logic behind what I do but also to see how it may affect what you do. You will likely scoff at some advice and find other a bit bewildering. Not many of you will have the time (or desire) to get into this depth of analysis. But I do think it will help you to be a better investor. Not that you will do what I do, instead I hope to give you some thoughts and ideas that will let you develop your own plan of investment. It will likely be far, far simpler than the one I use. It should be. You do not have the time to do what I do. Nor will you likely achieve the 25% return that is my target. Before getting turned off by that target this book will explain why I reach for (if do not achieve) that goal. If you read to the end of this book it is my hope that you will find you can put together a relatively simple plan of action that will produce hopefully good investment results for you. Now we turn to inflation as taxation.

From the beginning of history governments have "clipped the coinage." They have repeatedly through history debased their currency to hide the taxes and debts quietly imposed on their subjects. Our modern government is no different, just a little sneakier!

After all it is the federal government in the U.S. that runs the printing presses and controls the money supply. It therefore has its hands solidly on the throttle of the inflation engine. Need a few more dollars for a barrel of pork? No problem. Just print more dollars.

Despite all the lip service about wanting to control inflation, the government finds a modest rate of inflation quite profitable…for the government that is!

That is why it is such a tough job for an investor to come out ahead after taxes and after inflation! For example, if you earn 6% a year on your money then about one-third will go in taxes if held in a taxable account. 2% of the 6% pays what we generally consider as taxes. This leaves you 4% after taxes. Inflation has since WWII consistently run (some years more, some less) around 5% annually. After taxes you had 4% but now after deducting for inflation (4% minus 5%) you have actually lost 1%. Put another way, if you started the year with $100 and earned 6% on your money then at the end of the year you would really only have $99. At 6% you have lost a full 1% of your money in one year, and you did not spend one thin dime!

It may take a little reading and rereading to fully absorb this point, but it is one of the most important points in this book! So go over it again until it is absolutely clear to you. **Depending on the current rate of taxes and inflation you must earn enough on your money to cover taxes and inflation before you can even start to think about making money.**

It amazes me how few investment manuals make this clear. Yet it is only after taxes and inflation that you make any money on your investments.

Even very sophisticated investment manuals, whose authors really know better, cite the results of a particular investment program and then in some footnote mention that it excludes taxes or inflation, or both! But investment results, whether expressed in dollars or percentages, are meaningful only when calculated on an after tax/after inflation basis.

Failing to understand this clearly and to measure your investments by this after tax/after inflation yardstick dooms the investor to long term failure. Without realizing it, wealth can slip quietly away while you think you are actually making money.

To help make this point let's look at a few specific examples. First, consider the formula that we will be using in these examples. It seems simple, and it is. But like many great truths its simplicity is deceptive.

CURRENT RETURN - TAXES - INFLATION = REAL RETURN

Using our example above in this formula, we see how earning only 6% a year on your money actually loses you 1% a year if taxes are one third and inflation is 5%.

CURRENT RETURN - TAXES - INFLATION = REAL RETURN

6%   -   2%   -   5%   =   - 1%

Using the formula again, let's assume your current return on money is 9% instead of 6%. Taxes will take a third or 3% and inflation stays the same at 5%. Plugging these into our formula you get the following results:

CURRENT RETURN - TAXES - INFLATION = REAL RETURN

9%   -   3%   -   5%   =   + 1%

At 9% current return you now have a positive 1% real return. Put another way you could spend 1% of your money each year and come out even after taxes and after inflation. This means, however, that if you had $1 million in capital earning 9% you could only spend $10,000 a year without eating into your capital fund! And $10,000 is hardly what most of us would consider as buying a millionaire lifestyle.

Consider now what would happen if you could earn 18% a year with taxes taking one third or 6% and inflation staying at 5%:

CURRENT RETURN - TAXES - INFLATION = REAL RETURN

18%   -   6%   -   5%   =   + 7%

Note carefully what has happened here. You doubled your current investment rate, from 9% to 18%, but what you get to keep has gone up 7 times! From 1% after taxes and inflation to 7% after taxes and inflation. Now on $1 million in capital your after tax/after inflation spendable income is $70,000. Definitely more like it!

The figures used in these examples were not just pulled from the air. 9% happens to be the long term average return on U.S. common stocks, while 18% is the long term average return of the smallest 10% of U.S. common stocks (riskier but potentially more rewarding). Tax rate at one third is also an average although this is an ever moving target and varies from state to state. Inflation at 5% is higher than the average for the last century, which runs closer to 3%. But in the 25 years up to 1991 5% was the average and with the piling up of U.S. debt since 2009 it is likely that 5% will once again be a good average to plan around.

While 5% inflation a year does not sound like much, it can be a disaster for your wealth unless you protect yourself. At 5% a year, inflation alone will cut in half what you are worth in just 15 years! Remember, that is without spending a dime of your capital.

The methods you will work with in this book are designed to maximize your after tax/after inflation return – your real spendable income. On a reasonable capital base, by applying these methods, you can hope to earn enough to live comfortably and do those things in life that are most rewarding to you. It will not be easy but you will not have to spend hours a day to achieve the results if you follow the plan discussed later in the book.

Before we leave our introduction let us cover a couple of final subjects. First, what is a "conservative" investor? Second, what is a "long term" investor? These are terms that are loosely used in the investment community; they deserve a little forethought before using them.

Ask most people what kind of investor they are and 90% will say they are "long term, conservative investors." Yet the way many invest fails to conserve their wealth and often keeps them from being successful long term investors. The cause of this failure is often the result of not considering … you guessed it…inflation and taxes.

Consider a "typical" conservative investor – a trust department customer. Retired, living off their trust estate, Mr. & Mrs. Conservative have a $500,000 trust estate. This is divided as follows: 10% ($50,000) in money market accounts earning 6%

interest per annum (not in 2009-15 but when inflation kicks in likely this return will approach 6% as it has in the past); 40% ($200,000) in government bonds earning 9% per annum (again, not in the most recent past where lucky to earn 4% but we will use rates in the last major inflationary period of the 1970's in this example) and finally the last 50% in common stocks earning on average (dividends and capital gains) 12% per annum.

The Conservatives withdraw $3,000 a month to live on. This, with their fully paid for home and their social security, meets their current needs nicely. But what is happening to their nest egg? Apply our formula and see for yourself.

CATEGORY   CURRENT RETURN - TAXES - INFLATION = REAL RETURN

Money Market	6%	-	2%	-	5%	=	-1%
Bonds	9%	-	3%	-	5%	=	+1%
Stocks	12%	-	4%	-	5%	=	+3%

Now we will apply these real rates of return to the capital amount that the Conservatives have allocated to each to see the annual dollar real (after tax/after inflation) return.

Money Market	10% x $500,000 = $ 50,000 x -1% =	- 500
Bonds	40% x $500,000 = $200,000 x +1% =	+2,000
Stocks	50% x $500,000 = $250,000 x +3% =	+7,500
TOTAL Real Earnings After Taxes & Inflation		+9,000
LESS Trustee Fees & Expenses (estimated at .05%)		-2,500
REAL SPENDABLE INCOME		+6,500

Since the Conservatives think they are making more money than they really are they have been spending $3,000 a month or $36,000 a year. Since their real earnings are only $6,500 they are using up their nest egg and doing so quickly. At this rate, in 14 short years they will use up their entire nest egg!

Look at what they thought they were making each year:

Money Market   10% x $500,000 = $ 50,000 x +6%   =   + 3,000

Bonds	40% x $500,000 = $200,000 x +9% =	+18,000
Stocks	50% x $500,000 = $250,000 x +12% =	+25,000
Total		+46,000
LESS Trustee Fees & Expenses (estimated at .05%)		-2,500
Taxes (Estimated at one third less Trustee Fees)		-14,500
Net Income After Taxes		+29,000

Looked at this way, it is understandable that the Conservatives thought that they were only using up a small part of their capital nest egg. Even if they withdrew only the net after tax income of $29,000, at a 5% inflation rate their capital base would be cut in half in only 15 years as would their income, in current/real dollars.

Mr. and Mrs. Conservatives are actually very aggressive in their trust investing! By law and by the nature of their customers, trust departments are limited in their investment activities. The problem lies not in the trust departments but in the overall economic, legal, and tax system in which they are obligated to work. Also the nature of their customers makes it difficult to get real economic return for their clients since most are risk averse by nature and want a "stable" return. What they get, unfortunately, is a shrinking capital fund unless their assets are so substantial that their current income needs permits drawing down less than the total current income, leaving enough to cover the ravages of taxes and inflation.

What about tax free investing you ask? That seems like a solution. Lots of people think so. Between 401(k) and IRA and Roth IRA accounts most middle class Americans hold assets in tax advantaged accounts. Analyzing tax free bonds may make you wonder if that is an answer. Let's say that a taxable bond currently yields 9% and a tax free bond of similar quality yields 7% and that it is free from federal (including AMT), state and local taxes. Triple tax exempt as the trade likes to tout these bonds. Ok, apply the formula.

CURRENT RETURN - TAXES - INFLATION = REAL RETURN

7% - None - 5% = + 2%

If 100% of Mr. and Mrs. Conservative's $500,000 were in these 7% triple tax exempts then their real return would be a whopping $10,000 a year! Less fees and expenses they would have $7,500 per year to spend without eating into their capital base or what I like to call "eating their seed corn." There is also no assurance that they can average a safe 7% return on tax exempts. For many years tax exempts yielded only 3%

or less. It was only in the high inflation years of the 1970's and 1980's that big returns were earned and the average return on tax exempts exceeded 7%.

Now there are tax exempt investments (or tax deferred investments) that really can help. The Roth IRA is primary among these followed by 401(k), traditional IRA, Keogh plans and others. We will cover these later. To me, tax exempt bonds for most people only fool them into thinking they are getting ahead.

You need a big – really big – pot of assets and not much need to spend just to stay even with what is traditionally considered conservative, long term investing.

What then do I consider true long term conservative investing? First, to me long term investing is a lifetime or even generational. I hear investment advisers talk about long term investing and when asked what they mean say "6 to 9 months." I have to wonder what they plan to do with the rest of their (or their client's) lives! Investing done properly is a lifetime occupation, not something for 6 months, 2 years or even 10 years. True, your objectives and needs over time will change, but the need to invest, to maximize your return from your investments, remains for your lifetime.

As for conservative, to me conservative means "to conserve." That means earning enough on your money to cover taxes, inflation, investment expenses and leave you with a reasonable amount to spend or reinvest. Going through all the hard work of investing just to pay your direct taxes and your indirect inflation taxes – that is the ultimate in public service!

What is a fair after tax/after inflation rate of return? Currently, I think that 10% real rate of return is about right. To earn this means that in a taxable investment you and I need to earn….well you figure it. You do it by turning our formula around somewhat.

DESIRED REAL RETURN = CURRENT RETURN - TAXES - INFLATION

10%   -   X %   -   1/3 X% 5%   - 5%

For those who are a little weak in their algebra I'll tell you that X% is about 22%. That's right, to earn a real 10% you will need a 22% return on your investment. If taxes and inflation change, and they will, then you need to adjust the formula accordingly.

One of the better on line tools that you should find helpful is from the Bureau of Labor Statistics (BLS). It lets you project backward and forward in time to see how inflation has affected the dollar. You can, for example, plug into this calculator returns from your portfolio to see what the "real" value has been. Or you can use it to test mutual fund returns. For example suppose you started with PIMCO Total Return Fund started in 1987 with $10,000 and today in 2011 it is worth $68,500. Inserting 2011 and $68,500 then calculating for 1987 you will find that in "real" terms the $10,000 has grown to $35,000 assuming this was held in a tax free or tax advantaged account such as a Roth or Traditional IRA or a 401(k). Using a financial calculator you will see that this is a little over 5% a year real return. For those interested in the calculation you put 25 years in "n", 10,000 in the "PV" (Present Value) and -35,000 in "FV" (Future Value) and let the calculator calculate "I" (interest). Of course if you held this in a taxable account your real return would have been lower. Here is the link to the BLS calculator to which we will return later in the book. This is probably the best site of its kind that I have found and it is invaluable as you test your performance against the ravages of inflation! http://www.bls.gov/data/inflation_calculator.htm For those interested in financial calculators I have found the HP series the best. I have used the HP12c for over 30 years. Also some of these are available on line although I will not list those since they change too much to be useful to cite although a search will likely turn up a useful one for you. I recently bought a Platinum edition HP12c and find it is super fast in calculations compared to my two older Gold models. Any of these will work fine for you.

Personally my present long term objective is a 25% annual current rate of return with reasonably safety. Some years I may make 50% or even 100%, but then the next year I could be down 40% or even more. It is the long term average I am looking for. To balance out the good and bad years I suggest that you test your return on 10 year periods, each year adding a year and taking a year away. Often smaller stocks (one key I believe to a long term successful individual program) will go through 5 to 7 years of a down cycle of under performance against other asset classes. You won't escape them all, believe me. So, it is your average that counts.

I recently finished the 2012 updated version of Kenneth Fisher's book entitled "The only three questions that still count: Invest by knowing what others don't" and I found it extremely useful. It echos many of the themes of this book although it also differs in many ways. For those interested in a good basic primer for a sophisticated investor they would find the time spent reading this book well rewarded.

As you will see, my conservative approach is to keep a large reservoir of cash in short term cash type investments to cover these down cycles and then use the balance to go for top returns. My objective currently is to earn 25% on the entire portfolio (cash and stock investments). This is a tough, but I believe achievable, objective. The fact is that you and I will likely not achieve a 25% result, but by targeting it we will likely do far better than if we had as an objective a smaller return. If you achieve 20% or 15% you will be doing far better than 99% of investors.

And in case you think that these values for inflation are out of date and never to be seen again a recent lead article in the New York Times (October 27, 2013) argues that inflation is too low at even 2% a year (the current target of the Federal Reserve) and wants to see inflation at 6% a year or higher for several years! Unfortunately for savers and investors there is pressure from the business community, labor and from one odd source lenders for higher inflation. Why lenders? Because they fear with low inflation or deflation homeowners have no equity in their homes and are under water with their home values less than their mortgage. Ah, but with inflation all is good. With those inflated dollars the homeowner can pay off that mortgage as they watch the value of their homes soar. And wages go up too meaning more taxes for the government and people thinking they are making more. And of course they will spend that money fast because it is declining in value so they will buy ahead creating demand for goods. And companies can raise their prices increasing their profits. And the national debt! No worry, just pay it off with worthless, inflated dollars. Who gets the last laugh now China? Ah, the glory days of inflation!

So it seems the genie is stirring in its bottle once again and the lessons of the 1970's are about to be relearned. Because once this genie is out of the bottle putting it back is nearly impossible and is very, very painful. Ask Germany which after nearly 100 years still lives in fear of the hyperinflation of the 1920's when workers threw their pay (three times a day) over fences to loved ones who took wheelbarrows of the near worthless currency to buy a loaf of bread.

So when planning ahead keep in mind that there are those that gain from inflation and they are once again stirring inside the beltway of Washington DC and the figures above for inflation and interest rates may not be so far out of line as they appear in 2013 and may yet return to haunt us. And of course taxes go up dramatically with inflation as people are pushed into higher and higher tax brackets especially in areas of the tax code not tied to a cost of living adjustment such as the taxation of social security benefits and the higher cost of Medicare Part B when incomes rise over non cost of living adjusted floors. Is it any wonder that Washington is licking its lips over stirring the fires of inflation? One can hope that like Japan they will fail to fan these flames but if history is any help sadly it is likely they will prevail.

As you will see, my conservative approach is to keep a large reservoir of cash in short term cash type investments to cover these down cycles and then use the balance to go for top returns. My objective currently is to earn 25% on the entire portfolio (cash and stock investments). This is a tough, but I believe achievable, objective. The fact is that you and I will likely not achieve a 25% result, but by targeting it we will likely do far better than if we had as an objective a smaller return. If you achieve 20% or 15% you will be doing far better than 99% of investors. Yes, I keep repeating this remembering my old Latin professor whose favorite phrase was "repititio et scientia mater" or translated means "repetition is the mother of knowledge." And I am also aware that some readers will jump ahead so to those who tire of a bit of repetition please keep in mind why I repeat some key items more than a few times.

CHAPTER 1   ACCUMULATING AND HOLDING WEALTH

1.1 INTRODUCTION:

In this Chapter we will be covering a very broad scope as background for our discussion of investment methods. Before getting to the methodology for handling specific investments it is necessary to consider how to accumulate wealth and once accumulated how to hold it. Seems simple enough – and in concept it is. Application you may find somewhat more difficult!

1.2 EDUCATION:

It may seem a bit odd to discuss education as part of an investment manual. But consider the fact that your store of knowledge, whether accumulated in school or in what was once called the "school of hard knocks," is the one asset, the only asset, that no one can ever take away from you. A thief can steal your property. A tornado, flood or other natural disaster can ravish your belongings. A variety of business or personal misfortunes can send you into bankruptcy court and take your money from you. A government can confiscate your goods or through bad policy can thrust you into hyperinflation, depression or both.

Through it all, your education, your acquired skills, these are yours for life. So the first asset anyone should acquire is the best education they can aspire to. Not just in school but in life-acquired skills as well.

1.3 CAREERS AND BUSINESS

This book is not intended as a career manual but some discussion in general is in order. From my observation, next to inheritance the way most major fortunes are made is through entrepreneurial business. There are managers of large companies that have done extremely well, indeed become wealthy, but as a percentage the number is small. Most modest fortunes are made by owners of smaller enterprises. Not everyone, however, is cut out to be an entrepreneur. Many have tried, failed and realized too late that it was not for them.

If you are really one of those capable of being an entrepreneur then great, you probably have a better than average shot at grabbing the gold ring! You also may go broke, and maybe more than once. You should be ready for that. Over two-thirds of new businesses fail in the first year. The dream of owning your own business, being your own boss, can be very intoxicating. Also that dream can turn into a nightmare for you. But, if you have the nerve, the persistence, the skills and maybe just a little luck thrown in you may be able to build an enterprise that will truly make you wealthy.

For several years I was an attorney for a Fortune 100 retailer traveling across the country buying and selling properties and businesses. The one constant that I saw was that the really wealthy were the risk takers. The ones that developed shopping centers, built up small retail chains that grew big or were sold early for large profits. Many who were officers of companies did very well financially but not nearly as well as those who were true risk takers and entrepreneurs.

I guess that deep in our heart of hearts we all have the urge to be the next Sam Walton of Wal-Mart or Bill Gates of Microsoft. Before leaping into the entrepreneurial fire though you should take a long, long look. Also the more you have before you start the more you should consider if it is wise to take this step. When you are young, with little to lose, taking risks is one thing. Later in life when you have accumulated a modest wealth you should think your decision through very carefully before risking all. Indeed, if any of my arguments touch a nerve with you then you are probably not temperamentally suited to be an entrepreneur. Those I have known who have been successful have had such a passion within them to do what they have done that no one, no argument, would have ever stopped them! Had they stopped and thought about it they probably would never have done it.

It is not my purpose to encourage or discourage entrepreneurship, only to point out that it is a way to great wealth…and great poverty.

1.4 INVESTMENTS IN GENERAL

You can make money from your skills and labor. The better your education the better chance you have of making more money from your efforts. You also can make money by starting or owning an entrepreneurial business. True this takes skills and labor too but it also takes a desire and determination and a risk mentality that is absent in most professions or occupations. You can also make money from investments, letting your money make money for you. We turn now to this third way of accumulating wealth – letting your money make money.

What kind of investments? There are all kinds ranging from collecting Ferrari automobiles to real estate, stocks, bonds or gilt edge Treasury bonds. And there is a whole lot more to choose from.

The array of investment options open today is truly bewildering to most of us. Fortunately there are many studies that give us an idea of how various investments may fare over time.

Before we look at these studies we should consider the element of "luck" (good or bad) in investing. As in most other aspects of our lives our investing careers will run into some periods of good luck and some periods of bad luck. Also, there is something to making your luck – good or bad. You can position yourself to be in line for good or bad luck and that is something we will discuss at some length below. No real investor has failed to make some bad investments although reading the books some have written you would think they never made a mistake.

The real test is in recognizing and cutting short the losses that occur in investments that have turned bad. We all have the need to rationalize bad investments, to want to wait out a downturn and get even. Emotion in investing is very real and you will need to understand very clearly your emotions and to harness them if you are to succeed where others fail. The trick is not eliminating emotional response (you can't) but to control that response. Just as with a bad temper, counting to ten before making an investment decision in an emotional climate is a good procedure. Whether it is to let panic get you to sell out your positions (usually at a low price) or buy because of fever pitch buying as in the internet bubble or housing bubble. To think you are above these emotions you are either a robot or have nerves of steel. Most of us are going to be affected by the emotional environment around us. We need to recognize this and be prepared to lean against whatever emotional wind is blowing at the time.

One final thought before we turn to various investment assets you may want to own. There are a whole lot of folks that make their money by selling you investments – from brokers to con artists. They know greed and other human weakness. The good ones can play your emotions like a fine violin and you need to guard yourself against falling prey to con artists or those seeking their gain from your misfortune.

Whether selling you gold (playing on your fears and greed together) or penny stocks (get rich quick) or life insurance (playing to your fears, conservative nature and natural protective instincts) or collectibles (playing to your need to own things and to greed) or rare coins, or whatever else is being peddled just remember that anything looks good when a good salesperson is selling it.

The vacation property, time share, sailboat, sports car, rare coin, all look like no way to lose propositions in the hands of a professional marketer. If you are to succeed in investing you need to be prepared to resist these temptations. Since you will have money you will be their prime target. Like it or not you are an emotional human being whose emotions can be manipulated to your loss and their profit.

If being forewarned is forearmed then arm yourself well against what can be certain disaster for your wealth accumulating plans!

1.5 INVESTMENT CHOICES

Before going any further I will tell you that, after considering the various ways to accumulate and maintain wealth in the U.S. today from investments, I have concluded that common stock ownership is by far the best method for most people.

So right up front you should know that this is my conclusion. I could just skip the other asset types and go right to my method of buying, selling and profiting from stocks. However, since in your lifetime you will be faced with those who will tempt you to hold some of your money in other types of assets, I think I should discuss the other investment assets. This way you can see for yourself why I have concluded that for the serious long term conservative investor common stock is your best chance to preserve and build your wealth.

1.6 REAL ESTATE

After the real estate bust of 2008 to ? most people probably are not terribly interested in hearing more about real estate. But there is a tremendous real estate industry in America and it will eventually recover and thrive again. Land ownership as a way to own and hold wealth is as old as man. As the Forbes article mentioned in the overview noted, the great fortunes of Europe were many of them based on land. Great fortunes have been made in real estate- and lost too (ask Donald Trump!). Because of our European and agrarian background, there is a great mythology surrounding real estate in the United States.

In recent years a great deal of money was made by owning real estate in California, Florida and New England and property sold at a fever pitch. Alas it was not to last. This was not just an American disease as the same thing was happening in England, Spain, Hong Kong and elsewhere around the globe. A house in the south of France sold for over 500 million Euros to a Russian oligarch. That was one house just east of Eze. Anyone who looked at the average income of those buying at inflated prices knew this was a bubble about to burst, and it did.

In the United States when the latest bubble burst many a homeowner found themselves sitting in a home that was worth far less than they owed, or at the very least watched as their home investment diminished or vanished. In the 1980's it was the Savings and Loans that took the brunt of the decline. In the 2000's it was the banks and all those to whom they packaged and syndicated loans taking their quick profits and passing the potential loss on to others. It was a financial game of musical chairs and a lot of the participants found themselves still standing when the music stopped.

Real estate can be very rewarding. But not as an investment in my opinion. Unless you are really knowledgeable, lucky and have the time to devote to real estate investments. To me it should be looked on as an entrepreneurial activity – not a pure investment. If you can take a piece of real estate – raw ground, rental property, commercial, etc. and make something happen to it, then you can profit handsomely. However, if you think you can buy and hold real estate like stocks or CD's or bonds, you had best be very, very lucky if you want to prosper.

In the second decade on of the 21st^d Century I do not see any real profit in simply buying and holding real estate. From the 1970's to the mid 1980's it was a great place to be and for a while before 2006 in the new Century it was a good place to be as well, provided you got out early. Let's look at what made real estate such a good investment in the 1970's and early 1980's and see if we think those conditions are likely to repeat in the early decades of this Century.

1. **High Income Tax Rates with Tax Benefits to Real Estate.**

Comment: Rates were lowered with the 1986 Tax Act and benefits for real estate sharply reduced, in many cases eliminated. This may ultimately be looked back on as the straw that broke the back of the Savings and Loans who were deeply dependent on real estate inflation. The 1986 Tax Act turned real estate from a favored to a disfavored industry.

2. Baby Boomers buying first homes and trading up.

Comment: This phenomenon is essentially passed. Especially after the late 2007-11 real estate bust. It will be a long time for them to regain confidence in real estate. Meanwhile the influx of immigrants, legal and illegal, may at some point provide a floor to real estate pricing and is a source of future demand.

3. Interstate Highway System and Population Migration

Comment: In the 1960's and early 70's the interstate highway system was completed allowing cities to expand to their "ring roads" with resulting out migration of population. Shopping malls, industrial parks, office parks, and more suburbs followed. In addition, spread of air conditioning allowed real growth in the sunbelt where the population could now live and work in comfort even when the temperatures rose over 100 degrees. As baby boomers retire many will relocate to warmer climates. While all of these trends are still in place the cost of gasoline to travel from distant suburbs to jobs will limit expansion.

4. High Inflation and Fixed Mortgage Rates

Comment: Because of the housing bust and the Federal Reserve decision to keep rates very low mortgage rates have come back to levels not seen for many decades. How long the bond market will allow the Federal Reserve to keep rates low is an open question and with inflation picking up the guess is not long. Many a homeowner (including the author) profited handsomely in the 1970's and early 1980's from a combination of inflation and fixed mortgage rates that made homeownership look like a good investment and not just a place to live and raise your family. Many a rising executive treated their home as another investment asset and banks joined in the craze by lending on "home equity." Recent turns in the marketplace have perhaps brought back some common sense and the realization that home ownership is usually not an investment. In the 1970's and early 1980's and again in the first decade of the 21st Century real money was made by buying the biggest home you could qualify for, mortgaging it at a fixed rate, writing off your taxes and interest against your highly taxed income and then sit back and let inflation and the demographic trends push your equity higher and higher. Then when you sold you were encouraged by the tax laws to roll your "investment" over into an even higher priced home to avoid paying any tax on the sale. Recent tax laws have changed this to some extent but many people continue to buy bigger and more expensive homes as they trade up. If you did sell and realized more gain that is tax free that sale is taxed at lower capital gains rates. Ah, the good old days! Gone for now at least, if not forever.

Of course there will always be a "hot" real estate area. There will always be a "lucky" owner on whose land is found oil or gold or a regional mall site. But, if you buy real estate with this in mind (unless you are an entrepreneur who can **make** the development happen) you would probably be better off buying lottery tickets! Sure, you may get lucky, but to me that is not investing. Investing is putting money to work where, if reasonable expectations are met, you will make a good return after taxes and inflation. Putting money to work hoping that luck will make you money is gambling, not investing…no matter what the salesperson told you.

So if you are an entrepreneur with a nose and talent for real estate then by all means give it a go. Just be aware that the 21st Century is not the 1970's or the first decade of this Century. Keep in mind too the disadvantages of real estate. Probably the biggest disadvantage is its lack of liquidity. It can be very hard to sell when you want to sell. If you ever need money quickly from your investments, your real estate is probably the last place to look. Getting a fair value from real estate can often take months or years from when you decide to sell. No calling up your broker, telling them to sell and depositing the proceeds in your bank account a few days later. Sure, if you have a line of credit set up in advance you may be able to borrow against your real estate but that will cost you. Real estate has a carrying cost too. Real estate taxes, interest on any money you borrowed to buy it, upkeep maintenance, insurance, etc. All these costs keep piling up even while you are looking for a buyer. Knowing the value of your real estate is also a problem. Sure you can get an appraisal, check what other properties are going for but the acid test is the net dollars you get when you sell and that you won't know until you actually sell the property.

For me real estate is going to be a tough place to invest money in the 21st Century although there will always be entrepreneurs who can do well in this arena. There will be money made from buying currently distressed properties. But for my money there are easier, and to my mind safer, ways to invest.

Finally, beware the pitch men and women who through books, television marketing or over the phone who tout the get rich quick aspects of real estate. Any other investment for that matter! Most of these will make real money – for the promoters! Lots of people make lots of money telling you how to make money. Some may be genuinely helpful – this book of course being one of those! Just be skeptical and careful.

True investing is difficult and part of the difficulty is avoiding the lure of the scam or the current "hot" investment. Who doesn't want to get rich quick, with no risk and no effort? Other than winning the lottery, striking oil or some other piece of good fortune it is just not going to happen. Yet every day I can find hundreds of get rich quick scams being peddled. Some are very seductive. They fool lawyers, doctors and otherwise savvy folks that should know better. The truth is that no matter how smart they are they are human. They have the same emotions of fear and greed that sets them up for the scam.

My bottom line advice is to leave real estate alone for your investments. Buy real estate to live in, to enjoy, to raise your family in. Just don't think of it as investment. If it turns out you make a good profit when you sell then great, just don't count on it.

1.7 COLLECTIBLES

Another area trading on greed and quick, easy money is the collectible craze. For some reason we all like to collect things: coins, stamps, dolls, baseball cards, plates, antiques, old cars, etc. As long as collecting is a hobby that you can afford then enjoy yourself. The minute you start thinking of it as an investment, think again! And turn off Antique Roadshow!

Yes, there are lucky people. The guy that bought a picture at a flea market only to find it was backed by an original copy of the Declaration of Independence, worth a seven figure amount. Or the fellow that bought a junked Ferrari, only to sell it later for millions. There is scarcely a field of collecting that does not have a similar story to tell. But this is lottery stuff. Some one has to win, might as well be you…the salesperson says.

Unless you have developed the talent to be a collector/entrepreneur you are not investing. Oh, the dealers will tell you that you are. That you have a real eye for value!

Judged by our yardstick of real return, current return after taxes and inflation, collectibles just do not hold up. There are times they will skyrocket in value but over the long term they tend to track right along with inflation. And they do not have the tax advantages of other investments. Perhaps their best attribute, along with real estate, is that until you sell them there is no current tax on their accumulated value. But when your chips are cashed in, unless you are favored by luck or truly have an unusual knack or knowledge – in which case you are entrepreneuring not just investing – you are not likely to come out a winner from collecting. One exception under current tax law is if you inherit a collection it may get stepped up in value meaning that if those leaving you their collection bought it for say $1,000 and today it is worth $100,000 then when you sell your tax basis (what IRS calls it) gets stepped up from $1,000 to $100,000 so if you sell for $100,000 then you pay no tax. Unless they change the rules of course. And if you are the one leaving your collection to someone this does not help you!

Take the spectacular profits reported in recent years from impressionist art. All the news shows have pictured the millions of dollars a single painting by Monet or Degas has sold for. Pretty spectacular? Not really. After taxes the painting that sold in 1990 for $20,000,000 and was purchased in the 1920's for $20,000 sounds fabulous. But consider the real return. The $20,000,000 is first reduced by one-third for taxes. That leaves $13,333,333. Not too bad so far. But over the 65 year period of ownership this works out to be an annual return on the original $20,000 investment of 10.5%. Taking inflation at 3.4% a year away and you are left with a real return of 7% a year. Good but not very spectacular. And how many other paintings were there that did not rise in value so spectacularly? Furthermore, we did not deduct the very sizeable costs of maintaining and insuring the painting, costs that would sharply cut into the profits.

Be careful thinking of collecting as investing. If you have the skills to be an entrepreneur/expert dealing with a field of collecting then real money can be made. Just be sure not to confuse being an entrepreneur/expert and an investor. The investor buys, holds and sells. The entrepreneur/expert adds an element of personal expertise and knowledge which creates extra value. The knowledge or ability to spot a neglected bargain, the knowledge or ability to buy in a low priced market and sell in a higher market, the knowledge or ability to be a "horse trader," a skilled negotiator. While being a good investor takes knowledge and ability it is not the skill of an entrepreneur. You must never confuse the two!

Collecting can be a lot of fun, even profitable. Be wary, however, of thinking of it as investing. As with real estate if it turns out that your hobby is profitable then great, again just do not think of it as investing.

1.8 GOLD, TREASURY BILLS AND OTHER "SAFE" INVESTMENTS

Viewed over a 120 year time frame, gold, treasury bills and treasury bonds have all had their day. Over the long haul they have all fallen short as ways to make or maintain wealth. The after inflation return of all three is essentially flat to slightly up or slightly down.

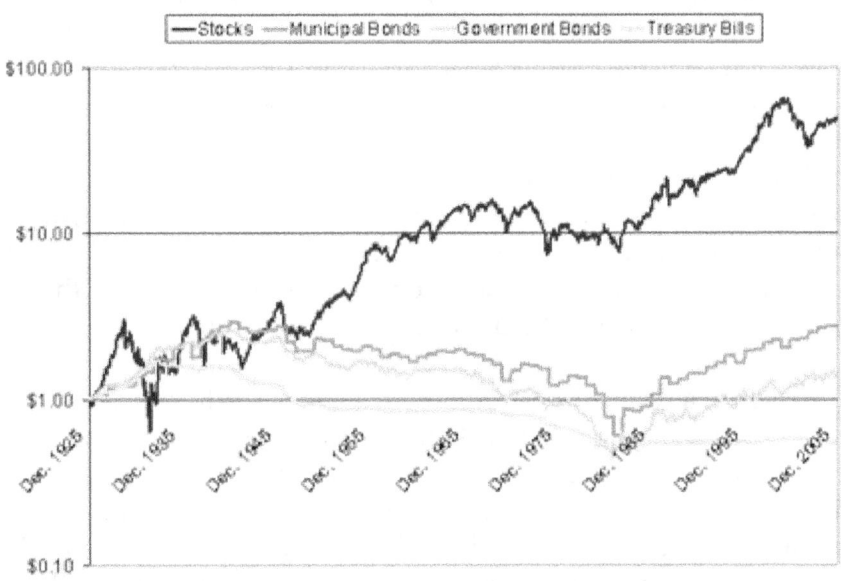

Stocks, bonds and T-bills after taxes and inflation. 1925-2005

Hypothetical value of $1 invested at year-end 1925, with taxes paid monthly. No capital gains taxes are assumed for municipal bonds. Assumes reinvested income and no transaction costs.

Source: Ibbotson Associates

Those who make money advising you or selling you investments may trade on your fears to sell you gold or bonds of Treasury bills. Gold, bonds and Treasury bills do have a place in a well organized investment program. The place for them is for short term holding and for your cash reserves to protect against stock market down drafts. One look at the long term performance should be enough to convince you that these are not the place to put truly long term investment money. These supposedly "safe" investments are safe only in the short term. Over the long term they are very dangerous to your financial wealth.

Recently after the financial collapse of 2008-9 TV ads have sprung up touting gold. Whenever you see ads like this just remember that they usually occur at the peak of markets. Just as you can recall hearing from friends not too many years back that you were foolish not to buy a house as an investment, that those who could buy and were living in apartments were foolish. Well, they do not look very foolish now, do they?

Beware the siren song of "conservative" investing just as you beware the siren song of the get rick quick scammers!

1.9 COMMON STOCKS

You probably thought we would never get here! After telling you my conclusion, that common stocks are the place to successfully invest for the long term, I have talked about everything *but* common stocks. Hopefully you will see why. You will be tempted on any number of occasions to abandon common stocks (and there are times it will be best to step aside temporarily) and the lure of other so-called investments can be very tempting. Just as a flu shot may protect you from the flu, it is my hope that a shot of common sense thinking with protect you from improper investing.

Look back at the chart in the previous section. You will see the 120 year history of common stock investing. As we get into the details a little later we will develop this theme and show how these returns are even greater for some classes of common stocks. For now it is important to note that common stocks seem to offer one of the few ways to possibly win in the race to be successful after taxes and after inflation.

There are major advantages to common stocks. Whether owned directly or through mutual funds or ETF's (Exchange Traded Funds, about more later). Liquidity is one of the greatest of these advantages. Most common stocks traded on a stock exchange can be sold and the cash banked a few days later. There are exceptions such as when stock exchanges were closed after the attack on the World Trade Center on 9/11/2001. In a mutual fund you may even be able to write a check the day after you sell. If you have to sell when stocks are down you will get less for your investment. And you will have taxes to consider, a subject we will also discuss in some detail. But you can sell and do so quickly. With the development of mutual fund families that permit you to move between various funds with a phone call or through the internet, the convenience of investing has increased.

There is also the advantage of knowing daily the exact value of your investment. Your local paper, The Wall Street Journal, Investor's Business Daily, or online with Yahoo Finance, CNBC or many other internet sites many of which give you real time quotes, all will give you current pricing of your stocks or mutual funds.

Of course there is risk. Risk that the value of your stocks will do down as well as up. But the fact is that the stock market over the long term has a positive upward bias of about 3% per annum. This simply means that even if you bought stocks at the worst possible time, provided that you bought a reasonably diversified portfolio of stocks, over a period of several years you would still achieve a profit. Of course, if you avoid the steepest declines and can buy into the market when it is relatively low, then your profits can be substantially better than average. While this is easier said than done, there are techniques we will be discussing that can help to smooth out the bumps along the road.

Before we go too much further I should mention that when we start talking about stocks in detail I will assume that the reader has some knowledge of stocks and investing. The techniques in this book, while of interest to the general reader, will be meaningful only if you have some reasonable grounding in investing. If you feel a little weak in this regard or if you are a true beginner then I would urge you to read one or more of the basic books on investing, before getting too much further in this book. The diversion will be well worth while for you.

Before we leave this initial survey set out below is a table showing annual rates of returns for various categories of stocks from 1927 to 1983. Nothing has changed since then to alter the relative returns. However, it is worth noting that the annual rate of return is over a long period and in that time there have been times when larger or smaller companies have performed better. But over time smaller companies have tended to have better rates of return. This material was prepared by Normal Fosback and published in his newsletter, Market Logic, as a research report.

NYSE STOCKS 1927-1983

Market Value	(Smallest to Largest)	Annual Rate of Return
1. Smallest 10%		18.2%
2		11.8
3		9.2
4		9.8
5		8.3
6		8.1
7		7.9
8		6.1
9		7.1
10 Largest 10%		4.7
Average		9.1

This table shows dramatically the increased rewards of focusing on the smaller stocks over the larger stocks. True, the risks are greater but so are the rewards. Calculated on an after tax/after inflation basis you could have come out behind even investing in stocks unless you focused on the smaller stocks or at the very least had a good balance of large and small issues. The American Association of Individual Investors (about which more later) has done studies confirming these results.

Were you able to "time" the market, get in stocks near the bottom and out near the top, you could substantially improve on these averages. One of the basic philosophies of this book is that long range timing is indeed possible and profitable and we will discuss easy ways of doing this. To achieve my 25% a year return it is necessary for me to focus on smaller issues and to do a certain amount of market timing. Not trading, certainly not day trading! Often the timing I am talking about will be 5 years apart, other than annual or semi annual rebalancing of a portfolio, so we are not talking about frequent timing.

While it is difficult to time the markets (no one can, by definition, anticipate Black Swan events – those events that are outside the expected e.g., wars, natural disasters of various sorts or financial collapses hidden from view) and you will never buy at the precise bottom or sell at the precise top if you can successfully engage in some market timing you will improve your performance. We will be going into these subjects in detail later. For now it is important to understand the concept of focusing on smaller issues and moving in and out of the market at extreme valuations – be they high or low. Because it is impossible to know for certain I use a rule of 75-25% where I am never more than 75% invested in common stocks and never less than 25%. No matter how certain I am of the market direction. For the busy professional I will be suggesting you consider investing at the 75% level in equities and use rebalancing to do your timing. Not trying to get in and out of the market. It sounds easy to get out near the top and in near the bottom but as we will see it is very, very difficult both academically and psychologically. Most investors do this poorly and their returns suffer accordingly.

There are people who will tell you that the stock market is nothing but a crap shoot, a gambling game, and that market moves make no logical sense. There are times you will be tempted to agree. Since the market generally anticipates moves in the economy 6 months ahead it can be moving up rapidly when you are reading in the news just how bad the economy is doing. Likewise when things in business around you are looking nice and rosy the market, anticipating a downturn, the market may be in steep decline. Because of this the stock market is used by ECRI (about which more later) and the National Bureau of Economic Research (the body that officially tells us when we are in or out of recession) as a leading economic indicator. What that means is that a move up or down in the market generally tends to happen ahead of moves in the economy. There are exceptions and one wag has indicated that the stock market has predicted 9 of the last 4 declines. And markets can rise in a bad or stagnant economy if the Federal Reserve is making money cheap enough (as has happened from 2009 to 2013 and projected to continue through 2014 and possibly into 2016 or longer).

The Value Line Investment Survey contains a wealth of information about stocks. It is available in most libraries and they offer reasonable trial offers. Even if you don't take the service it may be useful to take a trial offer from them so you will have available to you charts and information they provide. Morningstar provides a similar service for mutual funds. Since I have no affiliation with either of these organizations or for that matter any organization I mention in this book I think it is important that I set out limitations I see.

My reason for mentioning the Value Line Investment Survey at this time is to show you one piece of research that they publish annually and which helps prove the point that the stock market is extremely rational from an economic point of view. Watching every up draft and down draft it may seem that the market moves in chaotic ways. The truth is that the market follows three basic and key pieces of economic data. These are earnings, dividends and interest rates. Value Line has created a regression formula with these three pieces of data plotted and when looking back it is easy to see that the market has indeed followed closely the formula they use. They publish this every January and I go to the library and copy it to keep with my investment charts.

Unfortunately the formula works well for an investor only in hindsight. Since we do not know until the year is over what earnings, dividends and interest rates will do, the predictive value of the Value Line formula is only as good as the data that they use as an estimate. However, this does not mean that the formula is useless, quite to the contrary. What it proves to me is that the market is quite rational when its behavior is viewed over a long period of time. True, in its hour to hour, day to day, week to week, movements it can appear to be quite contrary to reason. Over time, however, its movement is quite reasonable and soundly based on economic success or failure of the stocks within the market.

1.10 OPTIONS, CONVERTIBLES, PREFERRED STOCK, ETC.

Since the 1980's there has been a wild proliferation of new types of securities. I suppose it is the computer that has made this possible. Doing the work by hand it was nearly impossible to monitor and create all of these bewildering instruments from ETF's to derivative and hedge funds, etc. I don't think that recent financial gurus are any smarter or shiftier than their predecessors, they just have smarter computer terminals.

This is not going to be a tirade against derivatives, hedge funds, program trading or other sophisticated instruments or trading programs. In fact, I think that the careful private investor can make use of some of these to his or her advantage. You just have to be out of the way when the sophisticated trader buffalos start to stampede. Native Americans used to drive buffalo off cliffs (bit safer than trying to attack them one on one!) and like the Native Americans we want to be out of the way when the stock market buffalos go over the cliff. We recently saw this phenomenon when financial institutions bought into the high risk syndicated mortgage instruments that destroyed a number of our venerable and older financial institutions such as Lehman Brothers, and nearly brought down a host of others.

No, the purpose of this section is to cover in summary way some of the various instruments that look like common stocks, act like common stocks and are often sold as common stock equivalents but which are not common stock equivalents.

Derivatives are instruments (of seemingly infinite variety) that use models to imitate behavior of whatever they are "derived" from e.g., a derivative of the Dow Jones Industrial Average might be an instrument involving counterparties (those who stand behind the derivative or in the case of Lehman Brothers end up not standing behind the derivative) who trade the instrument. With computers traders are able to slice and dice bonds, stocks and other risk instruments into a plethora of products. For example they can take a Treasury bond of 30 years and slice it into various maturities, interest only or principal only (called strips). While some of these instruments are not truly derivatives they tend to operate the same.

Another product is the ETF or Exchange Traded Fund. Again this can appear to be similar to common stocks but may or may not involve the fund actually owning stocks. These ETF's may involve derivatives, options or a host of other esoteric forms and those buying ETF's need to understand clearly what they may be buying and what risks they may be taking. The ETF world has exploded in the 21st Century. There are funds for gold, silver and variety of commodities. There are funds for US small capitalization stocks and funds for large capitalization stocks. Funds for energy, technology, medical care and for US stocks, Brazilian stocks, regions of the world, etc. so that investors can pick and choose if they feel that particular investment vehicles will do well or poorly. For the busy professional, manager or other person without time or inclination to manage their investments these ETF's will only occasionally be useful to them. If they use 401(k) investments most of these will not even be available to them. In an IRA on the other hand, Roth or Traditional, they may make use of ETF's. Indeed the gold ETF's may be the best way to hold gold if it is felt that is advisable or useful.

In addition to these products we have options on options, futures on options, options on particular stocks, stock indexes or commodities. Long term options, short term options, instruments that strip out the capital gain portion of stocks, options that go long, options that go short and the list just keeps expanding.

There are times when the true conservative long term investor may want to look at these instruments. But, frankly, I have looked at most of them and they are best left alone for most investors. Not only do they confuse, but they appeal in many cases to the speculative/greedy part of our souls. Most involve leverage (which is borrowing and magnifies both gain and risk). This means you can lose more faster or make more faster.

Faster than with the underlying common stock (or whatever the underlying security may be). For the most part I do not believe in leveraging in the stock market, whether buying on margin (particularly dangerous) or through options. For those fully versed in their use and who have the time and inclination there may be times these will be useful to a conservative long term investor. But not many! And if your objective is to simplify your investing you should know about these but almost always avoid them. I have tried and tried to find a use for these instruments in my own investing but have come up dry. There are plenty of uses, I just cannot find a profitable use that does not involve unacceptable complexity, cost or risk.

You may be tempted from time to time by one or mores of these instruments. If you study my methodology carefully, I think you will find that they will only take you away from a path of successful investing. Most are either for the speculator or the specialist. For example options on currency futures. This can be very useful to a corporate treasurer who needs to time the bringing of monies from overseas back to the U.S. or the other way around. Or to hedge against currency fluctuation. If you do international investing on a large scale this may work for you too. If you are a small player (say $10 million or less in overseas investing) then you will likely find that the cost and complexity of hedging will exceed any benefits.

Preferred stock is another example. Because of a peculiarity in the Federal tax code allowing a dividend deduction between corporations where one corporation owns stock of another, corporations often buy preferred stock in other corporations. The preferred may or may not be convertible into common stock as a convertible bond may also be convertible into common stock. What the corporate owner gets is a dividend deduction and generally a larger dividend than on the common stock. Say you are a corporate treasurer with some spare money sitting around for a year. Maybe you are building a new plant, have set the funds aside from a new bond issue and will not need to pay for the plant for a year. You could buy treasury bonds yielding (not today but over time) 9%. If your corporate tax rate is one-third that would leave you with 6%. Deducting inflation at 5% (again not at the moment but likely soon!) you are left with a positive 1% at the end of the year. Or you could buy preferred stock. Let's say Giant Industries, a triple A credit (of course after Lehman and General Motors failures one wonders about ratings) which has a preferred issue yielding 9%. Under the old tax law the corporate treasurer could buy the preferred paying only 1% in tax rather than 3% and at end of the year sell the stock (assumes neither gain nor loss which is a risk(and have a net after tax and inflation of 3%. Triple his fully taxable investment. Of course there is some market risk, but often by choosing the right preferred this could be minimized. The point of telling this story is that the use of preferred was mainly for corporate treasurers. But you will see these issues listed in your newspaper and some are purchased by individuals.

One aspect of preferred from whence its name is that in event of bankruptcy preferred stock will be preferred over common shareholders when diving up the carcass of the defunct corporation. But they come behind creditors and in modern bankruptcy creditors generally do not come out whole meaning that there is nothing left for preferred or common stockholders. So while legally preferred stock has an advantage as a practical matter it does not. There are times when it pays a higher dividend than common and some have a conversion into common stock. So there are occasions when preferred even for an individual might be a better buy. But once again unless you want to spend a great deal of time and effort a focus on preferred stocks is not generally an investment you should consider.

What I have just said will be heresy to many who think that all the various optional instruments have a significant place in the investing universe. For the professional I would certainly agree. But for the busy person I just think that they divert attention from the long term goal. If these instruments make sense for you in a particular application then be my guest. Just be sure that they are not just smoke and mirrors and that your overall return, after expenses, taxes and inflation meets your objective. And do not be dazzled by mathematical models or fancy tricks that occasionally fool even the most sophisticated. As those that bought syndications of junk mortgages thinking that by pooling large amounts they were mystically converting lowest grade investments in to highest grade investments. The modern form of alchemy. And alas the Alchemists failed to convert lead into gold and so did the syndicators of these products --- except for themselves of course.

As for me it is complicated enough just dealing with market timing and common stocks, without adding another layer to deal with. So if you are looking for a detailed explanation of the new and sophisticated instruments I am afraid you will have to look elsewhere.

1.11 CONCLUSION

There are many ways to accumulate and to hold wealth in the United States today. What you must do is to fit these ways to your own talents and personality. But whatever choices you make be certain that you test the results against the formula that will tell you if you are successfully achieving real return, after taxes and after inflation, on your efforts and investment.

Part of your success will be to simplify what you do. That is one of the reason that I stayed away from complicated tax shelters in the 1970's and 1980's and from the sophisticated strategies of today. I had a chance to become a "name" at Lloyds of London twice in my investing life and both times felt the risk was too great, as many found out when Lloyds effectively collapsed in that form only to be reborn with more limited liability. Prince Charles second wife found out the dangers being wiped out in the process. And she was not alone. I would rather place my reliance on the long term trend of the common stock market and develop a strategy that lets me maximize my return from following that trend. The old adage still applies. If it sounds too good to be true then it most likely is!

CHAPTER 2. STOCK MARKET 101 – EFFICIENT MARKET VS. ?

There have been innumerable academic studies made of the stock market. One, in particular, has had considerable impact. That is the academic theory of the efficient market. What this theory says, in plain language, is that current market prices reflect all the knowledge that is in the market today. In short, none of the usual analysis, fundamental, technical or otherwise is worth a hoot in picking your stocks.

According to this theory you would be better off simply picking a diverse group of stocks at random than in trying to select stocks based on analysis of their fundamental or technical trends.

Some call this the dart board approach to picking stocks. Indeed the Wall Street Journal at one time published a column every so often comparing their "dart board" random selections against a group of so-called professional investors.

Perhaps more importantly there is large amount of money sitting in very large investment pools, from pension plans to life insurance reserves, that is invested using this theory. What many of these groups do is to simply give up trying to beat the market. Instead they invest in the stock market indexes themselves through an Index Fund, an ETF designed to mirror the index of their choice or create their own portfolio designed to mirror an index. One of the most common indexes is the Standard and Poor's 500 index which is an index comprised of 500 large companies that is the standard measure of professional money management performance. Indeed it is surprising how few money managers have been able in actively managed funds to do better than the Standard and Poor's 500 index. Some do well for a year or several years but then fall back and do more poorly for a time. Some 80% of actively managed open ended mutual funds that are designed to beat this index have failed to do so over long periods of time. The result has been the creation of index funds. Fidelity and Vanguard are two mutual fund companies that offer such funds.

First let me say that I agree generally with the Efficient Market Theory. But not completely. If I were a pension fund manager, or the manager of a billion dollar pool of assets of any type, I would probably be sorely tempted to use the index approach. As the size of assets under management grows it becomes more and more difficult to "beat" the market. Indeed, with a very large fund to some degree you ARE the market! To buy a stock that will significantly affect performance of your fund you must buy and sell such quantities that your ability to time your purchases and sales becomes extremely difficult without moving the market to your disadvantage. Which means that you have to buy very liquid stocks which in turn means megacapitalization stocks. And as we saw in the table in the previous chapter these are the one that perform least well over time. So if you are a large professional manager why not simply take advantage of the upward bias of the stock market and be happy with an index average.

The reason I would not be happy as an individual (as opposed to a manger on a salary basis of a pension or mutual fund) is that the market average will not produce a satisfactory return after taxes and inflation. A 9% pre-tax, pre-inflation return is worth only 1% after tax and after inflation, as we have discussed. So accepting an index approach for an individual, taxable investor is not the same as a pension plan that is not currently subject to tax.

Also, there are a number of studies, Value Line, Market Logic, AAII and a host of others, that show that you can do better than the averages with a variety of investment strategies. We are talking now of the individual investor, with thousands or perhaps millions of dollars to invest. Their purchase can be in stocks that the big investors avoid, or only dabble in, and in smaller stocks that historically have produced superior returns.

If you want to read about the efficient market theory and about portfolio theory in general take a look at "The Stock Market" by Lorie and Hamilton. It is a bit technical but interesting reading.

The main point to remember is that there are a lot of vary smart, knowledgeable professionals who spend their careers trying to do better than the market in general. And very few of them are successful! And those that are may be for a period of time and then underperform for a period of time. Fortunately for them, outside the academic and professional investment world very few people are knowledgeable about the efficient market theory. Among those who are knowledgeable most feel in their heart of hearts that it just cannot be true. With knowledge and skill surely you can do better than simply throwing darts at a list of stocks. I am among those who feel that way, but I have to admit there is a lot of evidence on the other side. So before you believe anyone who says they can beat the market view their claims with great skepticism.

Whatever you do don't let short term performance convince you that a particular style of investing is successful. Over a period of 5 or even 10 years some pretty odd-ball theories have "worked." Probably the greatest example of this are those who gamble in commodities. Many a player has seen his fortune made, then lost, then made again, then lost again, with the heart pounding moves that various commodity systems produce. The fact is that 80-90% of the commodity players lose money and eventually leave the game. Just like at the casino you can have a great run of good luck. Bet on black at the roulette table and if it comes up 6 times in a row your pile of chips will grow impressively. A $2 bet will grow to $64 in just 6 lucky spins. That is a 31 fold increase. 3100% gain in just a few minutes. Wow! And if we extend that same rate of return to annualize it...well it is umpteen godzillion dollars! But bet your stack of chips once too often on black and eventually it will come up red. So much for your godzillions of dollars! Every mathematician knows that the odds at any casino favor the house – that is how they make money and stay in business.

If you think this is a ridiculous example, read some of the investment literature. You will see that this is exactly the kind of hype you are exposed to. XYZ fund has produced a 1500% return in the last 5 years. ABC has grown 66 fold since 1968, etc.,

etc. Just be sure to take out your calculator and find out what the compounded per annum growth rate of those investments has been. Has this been over a 25 year period? If so, was the return the result of one or two or five spectacular lucky years? What is the chance of repeating this performance. Many an investor has looked a the winning mutual funds of the previous year and decided they were where they wanted to be for the next year only to be sorely disappointed as that fund's performance returns to the norm. They don't put the fine print warning that "past performance is no guarantee of future performance" without good reason!

I can show you investment after investment, from gold to penny stocks to impressionist paintings, to …well you name it…that over a 5 or 10 year period has performed spectacularly. The problem is that over a 20 or 40 year period all of these impressive gains tend to collapse. And by the time you have spotted one of these "hot" prospects usually most of the gain has been made.

For me, I prefer to stay with what has been successful over extended investment periods. There will be times I look with envy at those making big bucks in the "hot" fad of the day. Who wouldn't want to triple their money in a few days or weeks! Remember the glory days of the internet fad stocks up to 2000? People made 10x their money in a few months if not a few days in some of these stocks. But alas it all came crashing down and the NASDAQ average of its top 100 stocks has years later barely made it back to half its high of 2000 and those 100 stocks were the big companies. Most of the smaller companies in which spectacular profits were made (and lost) have disappeared. There are very few investors, if any, that can play this game with any consistent success. Very few take their chips off the gambling table or the stock market and walk way.

In the next two chapters we will be looking at various approaches to the market that attempt to beat the efficient market. The first of these two chapters will discuss the gurus, which is a term (not necessarily of endearment) applied to various investment advisors who publicly peddle their investment advice, mostly through newsletters but also on the various business TV channels from CNBC to Fox Business. Since I use several of these I am not knocking them. What I will be doing with you is to look at them with some skepticism. Remembering that they make big dollars selling you advice, whether it is good or bad advice, you have to consider where they are coming from in the advice they tender. After all, it is your money at stake, not theirs! True, if they are successful that means more subscribers, maybe a mutual fund they can syndicate and manage (for a fee naturally), and lots of talk show appearances. Most even have books they have written and will give to you for a trial subscription to one or more of their services. And many will have an on line or telephone "hot line" that you can log on to or phone to get an update between issues.

The next chapter after the gurus will discuss market timing. A number of services will offer advice on market timing. Since I believe that a limited amount of market timing does make sense for the individual investor I will try in that chapter to separate the wheat from the chaff.

My reason for summarizing the discussion of the next two chapters is to compare and contrast the approaches of the gurus and the market timers (a select part of the gurus) with the efficient market (dart throwing) approach to the market.

Before we leave this subject I want to be sure that you understand one thing. By mentioning "dart throwing" I am not intending to take the efficient market theory lightly. Only to make it clear with a simple, graphic and often used way of expressing the randomness of the theory. There is nothing wrong with a random sample selected from a group of stocks in forming a portfolio; dart throwing if you will. If in fact the market place does efficiently price stocks, meaning that the current price reflects much, if not all, of the information in the market about a stock along with its relative risk, then a random selection does make sense.

While I believe the efficient market theory has some important flaws, applied to the individual investor, I take it quite seriously and so should you. If, over time, you find that you cannot beat the market index averages with your own styles of investing, then by all means consider an index fund for your investing. You are not limited to large cap funds like the Standard and Poors 500, instead you can use several indexes including foreign stocks, small cap stocks, etc. in order to develop a portfolio that gives you more of a balanced approach. There are plenty of funds and ETF's for domestic and international indexes, large and small stock indexes and a variety of specialty indexes. You can even do some market timing and likely improve on the indexes themselves.

Keep in mind that there will always be times that index funds will do better than the average investor. Just as in the casino, there will always be someone at the tables that is winning. After all that is what keeps the players coming back. But the test is over the long pull, not just a few months or even a few years. Also, remember that one reason pension managers use the index, efficient market, approach is that is a great job protection for them. They will never do better than the average but they will also never do much worse. Baseball managers and pension fund managers are both fired for poor performance, very seldom for average or mediocre performance. True, the big bucks go to the winners. But the pink slips go to the losers.

Playing the average may seem a sensible and safe approach for a salaried pension manager with kids to raise and a mortgage to pay. Can't exactly blame them and in their shoes we would likely do the same. Since they have a very fancy academic theory to support what they do plus a wealth of world statistics showing how few active managers (those who pick stocks to beat the averages) do better, they are on pretty safe ground. All they have to do is sit back and change some stocks when stocks are added or dropped in the index and make their additions and withdrawals at the right times. Not a bad day's work.

If you are satisfied with a 1% real return on your investment over an extended period of time then this may be for you. An index fund, efficient market approach may also be good for you if you are satisfied with a 6% a year return in your IRA, or other tax protected investment fund. That is 6% a year while the money is accumulating, since,except for a Roth IRA, the tax is only deferred on these investments until you start taking money out. While this will probably increase your long term real return (after taxes are paid at the end) from 2 to 4% per year but it is still not a wealth builder. And the actual rate will depend on how long you leave the money in a tax protected account and the rate of tax at the end.

While I believe you can do better than the efficient market theory suggests, be sure that you test your own investment results against what an investment in an index fund would do for you. One way of doing this is to open a small index fund account, with the minimum investment permitted. Then when you chart your performance you will run a chart of the index fund along with your other investments to compare performance. You can do this on paper although you will have to take into account reinvested dividends and capital gains which makes doing this by computer far easier. If the minimum investment account is small enough using an actual account with say $1000 invested in it useful. If you add to your other investments, however, you will need to add a proportional amount to your index fund at the same time to keep the comparison accurate. And if you have both tax protected and taxable investments you may need two funds, one held in the tax protected account and another for taxable investments. This can get a little messy but it is worth the trouble to give you an accurate comparison with how you are doing versus the pros. If you are beating the index fund over an extended period of time of 15-30 years then you are doing well. It may not be an acid test, but it is a good one.

As an example of how things change quickly the phenomenon of the ETF (Exchange Traded Fund) is affecting the efficient market. Because hedge funds and computerized trading systems use these vehicles they buy and sell these vehicles quickly and in quantity. Since the ETF is an accumulation of stocks in a category of the market this can mean quick movements in not only the ETF but the underlying stocks. So in times of sale this means good stocks get thrown out with bad. And when being bought then bad stocks are bought as well as good ones. None of this has anything to do with the particular companies so their stocks are not reacting to news or fundamentals only to trading patterns. It is possible for a careful investor to use these opportunities to buy stocks unfairly beaten down because they are being dumped as part of an ETF or if they hold some stocks that have turned "bad" to dump them when the ETF is buying. This may be one of the few exceptions to the efficient market.

CHAPTER 3. STOCK MARKET 201 – GURUS

3.1 IN GENERAL

What is a guru? As the word is used today in the investment world it is someone who publicly advises investors and is considered an expert. Remember the tongue-in-cheek warning about experts – that they are people more than 50 miles from home who charge a fee! There are real experts, then there are people 50 miles from home. Telling them apart may not be as easy as you think.

I am going to include the mutual fund industry in the guru category. Why? Because these are institutional gurus. Some are run by by specific managers. The more successful ones, like Fidelity Magellan was for many years, will put their successful manager (Peter Lynch in that case, now retired) forward for public acclaim. Others operate by faceless committees or use computerized investing. Whatever their technique they hold themselves out as expert investors, capable of doing with your money better than you can do by yourself.

One thing about the mutual fund gurus that makes them different. Most have a "family" of funds that you can move between, often with the click of a mouse or a phone call. This is truly a great development for the average investor. What is not so wonderful is the "no lose" family approach. No lose for the fund that is! Many of the larger funds have such a wide array of funds that they are bound to have a winner in the bunch. No matter what the market is doing. Needless to say it is that winner that gets the advertising attention for the next year. Forget all the others. By having a series of funds invested in all sorts of assets, domestic, international, gold, zero coupon bonds, short fund, etc. and they are guaranteed that during any market period one or more of these funds is going to be doing quite well. So when you are judging mutual fund families be sure to study all the funds and their performance not just the latest winners. Compare their bond fund performance against other bond funds similarly invested. Compare high growth stock funds against high growth stock funds of other managers. In short compare apples to apples and oranges to oranges.

3.2 NEWSLETTERS

Most of the gurus write newsletters. Also many have a mutual fund or family of funds that they manage that attempts to apply their recommended strategy. A lot will have on line access and phone hot lines to get updates between newsletters. The short term trading gurus, who can change course in a matter of minutes if not hours, have a continuous hotline service that you can call during the day for updates. With computers that continuously update real time information and analyze data there is all kinds of opportunity to try to find ways to lead you to stock market profits.

In reading market letters there are several things to remember. First is that the newsletter writer makes his or her money off selling subscriptions or fees for managing their mutual funds, or in most cases both. True, if their advice is lousy you will probably not continue subscribing. And those that make good market calls will get lots of new subscribers. Indeed those who are highly rated by Hulbert, an independent who studies and ranks the various gurus on the basis of their performance, will get lots of new subscribers. And Hulbert himself has a newsletter type of service that if you find you are interested in newsletters is worth considering. http://store2.marketwatch.com/index1.htm As with many newsletters you can get free or nearly free trials. Newsletter writers might not kill for a good Hulbert rating, but they can sure get killed by a bad one.

And newsletters can make big money, really big money, for those that are successful. We are talking seven and eight figure money. Not for you but for the owner of the newsletter.

Newsletter gurus seem to have a hard time saying they goofed. Some are better than others. Most will admit to small mistakes, makes them seem human and almost humble. But very few will tell about their major disasters. Joe Granville, one of the early technical gurus had a wonderful run of success in the 1960's and made a big name for himself. Then he got into predicting earthquakes and other strange things and his investment advice got a little strange too. The result was that in one period an investor following his advice would have lost big bucks. Since then Granville has moved to Kansas City and has been doing well again. I just hope you were not one following his advice when he had his cold streak.

That is another thing. These guys tend to run hot and cold. Like dice players sometimes they have a hot hand and other times they (or more accurately their followers) crap out.

Even the best services and newsletters can lead you astray from time to time. For many years I subscribed to the Value Line Investment Survey. I still read it at the library since my current use of the service only takes a few minutes once a month. The statistical data available in Value Line is truly outstanding. They produce wonderful charts including some showing how successful you would have been had you been invested in their number 1 ranked stocks and stayed away from their number 5 ranked stocks. Oh yeah! Then why have their mutual funds not out performed the market? If is so easy why can't their funds succeed in achieving the same results?

Now don't get me wrong, their mutual funds have done reasonably well, just not as well as their chart of number 1 picks would lead you to believe they should be doing. Why does their performance fail? I am not really sure. I think the problem is the same that I have with a lot of other services. Unless you follow the advice exactly, buying every recommendation, which in Value Line's case is a whole lot of stocks (more than the individual investor could reasonably be expected to buy) you will miss the one stock that performs outstandingly well and causes the outstanding performance. One time I went through and selected 20 different portfolios of Value Line number 1 ranked stocks, randomly selected. The result was a wide variation in performance. So simply picking

10 or 20 stocks at random from their 100 number 1 stocks would not have guaranteed that you would have matched the performance of all 100. All it takes is one lousy stock in the group you picked or one stellar stock in the ones you did not pick to throw off your performance vs. the 100 stocks.

I am not trying to pick on Value Line. I think they have a wonderful service that is extremely valuable. But I do caution you in using their service. Even more caution is needed with other services.

In the remainder of this chapter I will talk about the gurus dividing them into various categories. Hulbert, mentioned earlier, who does his own newsletter evaluating newsletters follows some 180 newsletters and there are many he does not follow. I try to point out the good and the bad about these services, why I use them or why I have used them and abandoned them. This is not going to make me many friends in that industry but I have tried to give you my honest opinion. Your opinion may be otherwise. That is what makes horse races and stock markets.

3.3 FUNDAMENTAL

Fundamental stock analysis concentrates on the statistical facts about specific companies, industries, economies or the regional and global economy. Fundamentalists are interested in things like earnings, dividends, book value and a host of other economic and business related facts. They are seeking to understand what the value of a company is in order to purchase stock when it is at a bargain to that value and sell when it is it no longer represents a value.

The classic text "Security Analysis" by Graham and Dodd is generally the rock on which fundamentalists build their theory. The Graham and Dodd approach is a valuation method. They seek to determine the underlying value of a security and then buy below that value. One of the most successful current U.S. investors, Warren Buffett of Berkshire Hathaway, uses this approach in companies he buys.

Today there are variations on the value theme. Some gurus favor the strict Graham and Dodd approach and have been quite successful. Others favor emphasis on one aspect of value over another. Some favor book value as a critical test. To others free cash flow is key. Still others low price to earnings multiples. And there are variations on the variations such as price to sale comparisons.

There is no question that fundamentals ultimately drive the market. As we saw earlier, Value Line does an annual study using a regression analysis (that is they "fit" a trend line mathematically to certain statistical data) that is quite accurate. But while accurate it is little good except as a rough judge of direction since the range of values it computes for a particular year are often hundreds of Dow points wide of the mark. Knowing that there is a 90% chance that the Dow will fall between 10000 and 12000 in a given year is useful, but not very! What it does for me is to demonstrate that over a number of years the factors of earnings, dividends and interest rates are ultimately what determines value.

Let us look at those three factors, earnings, dividends and interest rates. They are used in the Value Line formula to determine stock price and the overall "value" of the market as a whole. As a stockholder you are interested in three basic things: 1) the price of your stock, 2) the dividend you receive on that stock and 3) interest rates on competing instruments. At any given time you could sell your stock and put the money in the bank or a money market fund, a short term government security or some other investment that will not fluctuate in value as widely as common stocks. Whether you choose to risk your money owning stocks will depend on the three factors above. When interest rates are high on a cash-type deposit or bond and you feel stocks are over valued you will be inclined to sell stocks and hold cash or bonds. On the other hand if stock values are low and so are bond and cash interest rates you will likely buy stocks. One reason the Federal Reserve has kept interest rates near zero after the financial collapse following the demise of Lehman Brothers has been to try and force savers into becoming investors and to take more risk. There is a constant comparison of what you can earn currently on stocks vs. bonds or cash. If you are able to earn only 3% on common stocks but 9% on money market accounts (as was the case in October 1987 before the market crashed 20% in one day) you may decide to hold cash instead of stocks.

Unfortunately in the short run the fundamentals are a tricky way to value stocks. Over time past history will show that at certain valuations common stocks are extremely good buys. For example when the Standard and Poor's 500 index yields over 7% history has shown that purchases turn out to have been well made. On the other hand when the yield is under 3% further price moves in the S&P 500 have been limited at best and often prices decline. Of course the interest rate on competing cash investments is a factor as well. The higher the interest rate at lower dividend yield the greater the risk and the lower the interest rate at higher dividend rates the lower the risk. In recent history return on money market accounts (except following the Lehman collapse in 2009) return on money market accounts and bonds have tended in the same direction as stocks. So when stocks are good buys so too have been bonds.

For many years, before the 1970's, a typical market cycle for an investor was based on the business cycle. Investors could make good returns by buying bonds near the top of a market, when interest rates had risen to a peak, holding them into the recession bottom and then switching to stocks. This cycle was based on solid economics. As the economy heats up in the up phase of a boom time interest rates rise on bonds. This occurs as the Federal Reserve (or other central banks globally) raise rates seeking to cool off the expansion. It also occurs because as the economy expands there is more and more demand for credit. And, like any other commodity, when there is more demand for the same supply this puts an upward pressure on prices (or in the case of bonds on interest rates). Stock prices on the other hand tend to lead changes in the economy by roughly 6 months. Sometimes more, sometimes less. As business people and investors look out in time they start to move not when the rain starts but when the storm clouds appear on the horizon. So stock prices generally begin to decline before business starts to feel the decline.

That is the reason so many people feel that the stock market is illogical. They see business booming and the market falls. Then they see business on main street falling and the stock market booms. Makes no sense, they feel. However, the market is looking not at today but tomorrow with tomorrow being about 6 months ahead. Now since no one knows for sure what tomorrow brings there are often many false falls and rises as investors try to guess where the economy is going and how it will affect particular stocks.

Later in this book when we talk about how to time the market to your advantage I will be suggesting that you regularly, weekly or monthly, follow two on line services that will help you to judge when to be invested in stocks and when to be more in cash. One of these is the ECRI weekly service, currently available free, that is a spin off from the National Bureau of Economic Research and while a private enterprise it carries on the basic leading indicator work of its founder. I have followed it for a number of years and it has an excellent track record of predicting economic cycle turns as well as inflation. Even their leading house price indicator has been excellent. They publish a book, available from them or Amazon or other bookstores, "Beating the Business Cycle" by Lakshman Achuthan and Anirvan Banerji that is well worth your time to study. They have created a "dashboard" which shows the state of the economy in a nice graphic form. This is updated for individual investors weekly at 10:30 on Friday morning eastern time. It can currently be found on their at the following link: http://www.businesscycle.com/ I will be discussing this at some length later but for now it is important to note that this is one of the two tools that I use in market timing and has proven its value over time. It is fundamentally based in sound economics.

Another service that focuses on fundamentals is Value Line. For each stock that they follow they create a line which they feel represents the fundamental value of that stock --- hence the name of their service. This line varies based on a number of factors. It is calculated differently for a utility stock where interest rates are more of a factor than for an industrial stock here multiples of cash flow is the common yardstick by which they value a stock.

Their overall analysis is quite a bit more complicated and to their credit they are quite forthcoming in setting out in detail exactly how they arrive at their values. So you can take a Value Line value and decide for yourself if you agree with their conclusions or not or make your own adjustments.

I use fundamental analysis only as a gauge as to where the market is relative to massive over or under valuation and to determine where solid value lies. If I can buy into the market at or below what I see as its long term value then I am comfortable riding out some of the roller coaster rides that the market will take. Later I will show you how I use long term trends in the market to determine what is good value.

For day to day or month to month decision making I find the fundamental analysis interesting but not overly useful. Where it does help is at market extremes. Infamous October 1987 is a good example. Some of you may recall that the Dow skyrocketed that year from under 2000 to 2720 before it proceeded to fall 1000 points in what has been the greatest one day crash to date in the U.S. stock market. What caused the crash? I'll give you my thoughts. In 1986 Congress enacted a Tax Reform Act that changed practically every rule in the book for investors. Real estate, which had been a heavily tax favored industry, was stripped of many benefits. Capital gains were stripped of their tax benefits too. Borrowing went out of favor since interest deductions were eliminated over time on consumer debt (as opposed to mortgage debt). Finally tax favored investing was dealt a death blow by sharp reduction in rates.

With all this change people who for years had poured investment money into real estate, tax shelters, etc., now had to find somewhere else to invest. At the same time interest rates that were double digits in the 1970's and 1980's had fallen into single digits. Trust officers were consoling their clients who were shocked when they rolled over the bank CD's only to find that their old 14% CD was now only going to yield them 7%. Of course in 2011 those rates sound fantastic as many CD's are yielding under 3%. Guess where that money went (as it is going now)? Part of it at least went into the stock market. Since many investors cashed in their stock market gains in 1986 to take advantage of the last of the low capital gains rates when 1987 came they were back in the market investing.

This demand pull started a stampede into stocks. Once the ball started rolling the market started going up and up and up. Based on the past trend of the market valuation of the Dow Industrials in 1987 the DJIA should have been around 1800 to 2000. At 2700 the Dow Industrials was excessively valued, whether you looked at the trend line, price earning ratios, price to dividend, price to sales, price to book. You name it and it showed an excess. The only problem in over valued markets is that they tend to get even more over valued, until something breaks. And break it did! Knowing that over valued markets tend to go higher and higher my own approach in 1987 was to set a point at which I would exit the market if the DJIA fell back to it.

Setting such points is tricky business and my own approach is to study where typical market corrections go and set my points slightly below that point. If the normal correction is exceeded in an overvalued market then it is likely that the market will break down to (and usually below) the long term value line.

In October 1987 I felt that anything more than a 10% retreat could represent the end of the excessive move. So I set my "out" mark at 12% under the market peak, or 2400 on the DJIA. Because of the violence of the down moves the week before Black Monday I exited the market on Friday before. Luck? Sure. But some skill too. True I gave up paper profits from 2700 to 2500 but I missed out on the moves to below 1700. Likewise when the down move became excessive I started back into the market at the

2000 level. By my calculations the long term trend of the DJIA crossed the 2000 level in January 1988 and I started slowly back in at that point.

My purpose in telling you this is not to toot my own horn for having "caught" the crash. I could easily have missed it. But the reason I was out when the big crash came was that my fundamental analysis identified the market as overvalued for most of 1987 and I therefore exercised greater caution while enjoying the gains.

I could have stayed out of the market entirely during the period of overvaluation, as many did. But my study of the markets shows that the greatest gains are made at the beginning of bull market moves, followed by another period of significant gain right at the end of moves. There tends to be a "blow off" phase when skeptics throw in the towel and begin throwing cash at the market. The trick is not to catch the top, if you do that you are one lucky investor! The trick is to set your "out" point to allow corrections to run their course with perhaps another up move to follow but be out of the market when the over valuation is at an end. And then not be tempted to move your target as it gets closer.

Having told the story of my success at spotting the top in 1987 I have to follow it with a big mistake I made in 1995. At that time the market appeared to be peaking and I lightened my positions. As I will advise later I have always kept a toe in the market even when convinced that markets will move down and always keep a toe out of the market when convinced markets will rise. This cash gives me a chance to correct mistakes. As a result of lightening in 1995 I did not fully participate in the incredible move from 1995 to 2000 showing that you can be hurt by getting out too early! There is an analysis I will be mentioning later called slow stochastic and moving average divergence convergence. Do not let the terms scare you. These tools I now use to avoid my mistake of 1995 and in conjunction with the ECRI leading indicators they are the two tools I use to time markets to determine when to be heavier in stocks or heavier in cash. Of course my being out in this period also allowed me to avoid the bloodbath that followed Y2K in the year 2000. I should also mention that it is much easier to move your positions if they are in tax advantaged accounts and you do not have to take taxes into account in making a portfolio decision. Again, more about that later.

My point in all of this is to show you that fundamental analysis can be extremely useful in guiding your portfolio but it is not the one factor that you can rely on. It is only one of several.

One more example before we turn to discussing technical analysis. In the 1970's there was a massive decline in the equity markets starting in 1973 and bottoming out in 1975. For those of us who were investing it was a demoralizing time. After two decades of good stock markets the decline was gut wrenching, not to say what it did to your portfolio. Many a portfolio that was fully invested declined 50 to 75% in this market. The DJIA fell from a peak of 1035 in early 1973 into the 500's before it was over. The average stock and the smaller stocks took an even bigger hit. We have just seen a repeat of this in 2008-9 with the financial collapse following the demise of Lehman Brothers.

During the bear market decline of both 1973 and 2009 many an individual investor thought that they saw the bottom of the decline and jumped back into the market. By the time the bottom actually came most investors had been tapped out. What they had to invest was invested. If so they missed out on one of the best up market periods in the Century.

The move from 1975 to 1979, particularly in the small stocks was spectacular. Before 1975 the small stocks had been written off by the investment community for years as they focused on what was called the "nifty fifty." Fifty big name, so called one decision stocks. Ones that you bought, put away and never worried about again. Not until 1973 that is! As the nifty fifty were pushed to astronomical PE ratios – 30-40-50 times earnings the smaller stocks were lucky to sport 10 to 15 PE multiples. Then it all collapsed. Much as the internet bubble collapsed in 2000. One difference was in 1973 everyone thought the big nifty fifty were safe.

Assuming that you followed the system I have suggested, moving some money out of the market when it is overvalued on a long term historical perspective (as it clearly was in 1973) when the market falls by 12% this would have gotten you out of the market around the 900 level on the DJIA.

By the way, I was not following the system back then. Fortunately I also was not fully invested when the fall came. But I had enough committed to have suffered with the rest. Holding on brought good profits eventually but not as good as they should have been. This was when I started really getting serious about developing a market plan that worked.

But that is an aside. My point is that I watched during this period as one after another of my friends succumbed to putting money into the market, at 900, at 700, at 600 only to see the market move lower and lower. Even when the market became undervalued, in 1974, it moved far lower than historical trend would have suggested.

As both of these stories illustrate, when the market begins its move it tends to overshoot "fair" value. The problem is how much it will overshoot. I find that this is where technical analysis is its most helpful. Once you have determined that a period of market over valuation or under valuation is occurring you need to consider that it tends to move much further higher or lower than anyone expects.

People in the market take quite a while to realize that they missed the move, they are always waiting for the correction to get even and get out. That opportunity almost never comes. When it does come it is usually at the start of the next major move and if they do get out they usually miss the important part of the next move. That is how not to make money in the stock market.

I find that technical analysis helps me in these time periods to buy or sell at points when I am comfortable. I seldom hit the high or low but I generally make bigger profits than simply saying the market is over valued so I am out or that the market is under valued so I want to be in the market.

3.4 TECHNICAL ANALYSIS

Fundamental analysis pays attention to underlying value. Fundamentalists are interested in a company's products, its competition, its management, its assets and most of all its free cash flow, earnings and dividends and their potential for growth. Technical analysis on the other hand, pays attention to the movement of stock prices, volume and other factors related to how a stock price or an index of stocks is performing.

The technical analyst may also focus on factors unrelated to individual stocks such as monetary factors or stock market sentiment. While not really technical analysis these factors seem to be given more play by technical analysts than by fundamentalists. Not that it matters to the investor who simply wants to know what and when to buy and sell and how to make the most profit.

It is not my purpose here to write a text on technical analysis. There are many fine books on that subject. If this interests you then by all means read more on the subject.

For our purpose I intend to focus on those technical factors that my experience has shown to be useful and on some that others think useful but which I have not found to be helpful.

My use of technical analysis is in two areas. First to define trends in the market, both long and short. Second, to time my purchases or sales. I do not use technical analysis to choose stocks or mutual funds in which to invest. And I certainly will not buy or sell merely on the basis of how a chart line looks or squiggles.

Where I do believe technical analysis has a place is to find turning points in a market or confirm the direction of the market. Later I will discuss the MACD (or moving average convergence divergence) which I find very helpful in spotting market tops. And I will discuss the Slow Stochastic measure which I believe is very helpful in spotting market bottoms. And I will discuss how I use this with a chart of the quarterly Standard and Poor's 500 average. But for now we will be more general in this discussion.

Whenever PE multiples have exceeded 20, that is when price is twenty times the prior year's earnings, on the Standard and Poor's 500 average, history tells us that this is a warning sign of over heating in the market. The market may go to 30, 40 or more times earnings before collapsing, but once 20 is reached a top is usually closer than a bottom. Likewise whenever the DJIA or S&P 500 yields more than 7% this has generally been an excellent entry point for purchases. Not that the market cannot or will not go lower. Simply that a few years out a purchase made at a 7% yield on these averages will usually be a very profitable investment. These are times to study the technicals watching for a turning point in the market.

One technique I have used is to plot the long term trend of the market from the early 1920's. This trend line for the DJIA runs upward at about 6% a year. Adding the usual 4% dividend this gives you a before taxes and before inflation annual total return of 10%. No guarantees, but the history is good. These can be very useful in forcing you to face whether the market is fairly valued, over valued or under valued. Like a road map long term trends give you an idea where you are at any point in time.

Another technique I have found useful is to watch the dividend payout of corporations. Generally speaking corporations do not like to cut dividends. So in good times they raise dividends cautiously. If in a period of rising earnings you see that dividends are not keeping pace it is a good sign that management of companies feel that the good news will not be continuing. The opposite works too. When earnings are falling but managements are holding the line or only slightly cutting dividends then they feel that earnings will be turning up in the near future. Now this test applies only with a group of companies. Some companies are more reluctant to cut dividends than others. And in a particular boom or bust period one company may be affected more than others. In the financial crisis of 2009 we saw this with a vengeance where financial companies were involved. And there were political considerations here as well after the bail out of these companies. So it is a group of companies that must be considered. I like to use the DJIA and S&P 500 for my test. Like most things technical, no one indicator should be relied on. They are like weather reports, useful but not to be relied on entirely. Especially the further out in the future you are projecting – either stocks or weather!

When we get into the specifics of the program I use to invest to achieve my 25% returns, I will discuss more of the technical indicators that I use. For now this section is merely to touch briefly on technical indicators as one way of looking at the market that is different from the way efficient market or fundamental analysts see the market. There are almost in infinite number of these technical indicators from point and figure chartists to Fibonacci number enthusiasts. And some of these are truly strange and we turn to one of those now.

3.5 ASTROLOGICAL

Believe it or not there is actually a newsletter that predicts market behavior based on movements of the stars and planets. It has even has gotten air time on CNBC etc. Amazing. Who knows, he may have something, though I doubt it. What it shows me is how desperate some people are for market advice.

It also shows one of the major shortcomings of technical analysis. Any economic analysis for that matter. There is a tendency to plot on a graph data and then compare that data to stock movements. When a correlation is found it is then touted as predictive. Well, simply because the movement of planets happens to coincide with movement of stock prices does not a correlation prove. No matter how many times the coincidence occurs or how perfect the "fit" of the data. This makes relying on true technical analysis equally difficult. How do you distinguish between genuine correlations from those that merely coincide? If I were to tell you that we had a fit between stock prices and trash dumped at your local landfill you would laugh at me. If I told you that I had a fit between interest rate futures and stock prices you would probably listen. But the connection may be equally wrong. Later we will discuss the Super Bowl Indicator to show just how wrong.

Simply because the one fit is in the same field of expertise (i.e., financial data) does not give it credence. Yet it is amazing to me to watch and see people put real money on the table because a particular chart has squiggled to what the chart reader (translate – financial astrologer) believes is a buy signal. If it is generated by a computer or an econometric model produced by a Nobel economist …well that is really sexy! It looks so professional. That is what Long Term Capital thought before its collapse in 1998 with a bailout having to be arranged by the Federal Reserve because it was so large that it threatened the global economy. And they had two Nobel price winners behind the curtain.

Those programs that update automatically as you are watching, taking their data off satellite and running it in nanoseconds through the silicon chips can be mesmerizing. The chart appears like magic with all sorts of fancy lines marking trends and such. And with a flick of the computer mouse you can produce incredible graphics. Wow! They even provide instant recommendations and analysis. All you have to do is point and click and the bucks will start rolling in…at least for those behind the curtain.

My point about this is to use common sense. I could sit here today and make a perfectly sensible argument to you that the market is going up. And I could produce facts, figures and charts that would be very persuasive. Then I could sit down in the next room with someone else and do the same thing – except proving to them that the market is going to go down. As a lawyer you would expect me to be able to marshal arguments and present a case on either side. But as a financial wizard, and expert, you would expect that I could divine and give you ultimate truth. Not so, not at all.

Consider this possible scam. The scammer mails out 100,000 letters predicting the market will go up and 100,000 predicting the market would go down. Then after a month they write the 100,000 to whom they predicted correctly and to half predict a rise in the market and the other half a decline. And so it continues until the final 1000 were absolutely convinced the scammer knows what he was doing and had the answer to stock movements.

This point was brought home to me in a wonderful way one morning watching one of the financial reporting channels, which will go nameless. At that time there were two, CNBC and FNN, which have since merged. Now there is CNBC US, CNBC world Fox Business, and Bloomberg available on cable and satellite. Government statistical data is usually released early in the morning and these services love to announce and give instant analysis on all of these releases. The day in question the release was on business inventories. This number is important because it shows confidence of manufacturers in the future of orders by building or reducing inventories, or perhaps shows that manufacturers are stuck with excess inventory they will have to unload before making new widgets. Anyway, back to the story, the announcer was on the air when he was handed the sheet announcing inventories. He proceeded to announce the figures and then engaged in instant analysis explaining how the decline would affect the economy and making predictions how this would affect the market when it opened. On and on . Then a hand reached into the screen and gave him another sheet. He then announced that someone had made a mistake in the prior sheet. Instead of declining inventories had actually increased. They put the wrong sign (minus for plus) in front of the number. To his credit he announced the change…though blaming it on some unseen and probably now departed staffer. To his discredit he failed to correct all of his instant analysis, which was of course all horse feathers!

All another reminder of the GIGO principal…garbage in, garbage out. Anyone dealing with computers knows that phrase. It applies in spades to financial analysis. Even if the input is accurate the analysis on what it means may be more astrological than you think.

At least the astrology services tell you up front that they are star gazing!

This is not a put down of technical analysis. Merely a warning that applies to relying on any so-called expert. What most experts peddle is their "opinion." Just because the expert says it does not make it so. Maybe through their education and experience they can give you better informed guidance but just as with your doctor, lawyer or accountant great care should be used in those from whom you take your advice.

3.6 HULBERT

If Hulbert did not exist someone would to invent him. We mentioned him earlier in the section on newsletters. What Hulbert does is to rank and rate various investment advisory services, principally newsletters. He reports these in his own service. He also writes a column regularly for Forbes magazine in which he highlights the ups and downs of various advisory services.

Hulbert's system is not perfect. But he is the closest thing around to an impartial reviewer. He tries to separate the wheat from the chaff and on the whole does a reasonable job.

If you study Hulbert you will see what a hard job it is to judge whether an investment advisor is doing a good job or not. Part of the problem is the time period over which you study performance. One year, five years, ten years, twenty five years? Some services do well on the one and five year time horizons but not so good on longer periods.

Then there are the new services that do not have a long horizon. How do you judge these?

My purpose of mentioning Hulbert is to let you know that he exists. That there is a service that studies other services to try and find the genuine investment guru and to find out the charlatans.

Needless to say those services that Hulbert favors with high rankings run his findings prominently in their advertising. And those not ranked highly? Well, they tend to have not so nice things to say about Mr. Hulbert!

3.7 ELECTRONIC GURUS, CNBC, PBS, FOX, BLOOMBERG & CNN

In the 1990's TV financial networks began to transmit over cable and satellite and have become a major source of investment news in a real time environment. For years before this development PBS aired the show Wall Street Week with Louis Rukeyser, which gained a substantial following. Many of the early stars on Wall Street Week went on to become recognized names in the investment game even today. Names such as Martin Zweig and Frank Cappiello.

Then in the 1980's CNN started an evening news show devoted to the stock market and daily news. PBS followed with their own evening report.

Neither matched the scale of the new financial networks which have continued to expand. FNN was the first of these and it later merged into CNBC which in turn spawned a European and Asian version CNBC World. Bloomberg has its own show as does Fox Business. By the time you read this there be even more of these (or fewer if some have disappeared).

These electronic gurus and number crunchers provide an amazing array of investment data and advice via cable, satellite and on line through the internet. Unfortunately they tend to provide so much data and advice, often conflicting, that there is a danger that an unsophisticated viewer may be mind boggled by it all. Confronted with conflicting views from all spectra the viewer is easily confused or misled. Also there the terrible tendency (as during the crash of 1987 or the internet bubble bursting in 2000) to convert these services into the financial news equivalent of CNN with all sorts of instant (and perhaps erroneous) analysis.

These new services are a tremendous help to the sophisticated investor, one that can sort through the various talking heads and listen only to those that have a track record making them worth hearing. And filtering out the rest. And the mute button is probably one of my favorite investment tools! As for the anchors they range from extremely talented to incredibly naïve. Some have real talent for analysis and others seem to have been handed cue cards and told to wing it. Some of the results are humorous (as with the case mentioned earlier were a negative figure was handed to the anchor instead of the correct positive figure and he proceeded to "study" the dickens out of the wrong figure) and other times not so funny.

As with any instant news program or instant analysis you should be extremely careful. First, the facts may be wrong. Even if they are right making fast judgments (even by qualified and talented experts) can be dangerous to your financial health getting you to do something you would not do on more reflection.

Especially to be avoided is to sit glued to the TV set or your computer screen absorbing all of the day's offerings. The mute button truly is a wonderful invention! Besides being mind numbing there is the risk of getting caught up in the emotion of the hour. Good investing comes from 1) sound economic analysis, 2) a solid investment plan, and 3) patience to carry out your plan. True, there are times you should act quickly. And in those times the information these electronic services can offer is invaluable. Especially those offering real time quotes. But listening to all they have to offer can result in considerable confusion. My suggestion is to watch and pick out those personalities that fit your investment plan and whom, after watching, you feel have a good track record looking back at their advice.

There are probably 15 or 20 personalities that are interviewed on these shows that I will sit up and take note when they are talking. Many of the others I instantly push the mute button. Unless you are prepared to be very selective in listening to these services I suggest you turn the sound off and just use the stock tickers and the financial information that is presented in the graphics, if you choose to watch at all. Often much of this is more easily obtained on line and in real time.

3.8 SUPER BOWL INDICATOR

When my daughter was in college I was looking through the catalog of course listings and noted one on formal logic. It reminded me how much I had gotten from this course in my own college career. The purpose of my mentioning this is my feeling that a good investor could do worse than spending a little time studying formal logic. Only if you know the fallacies in reasoning can you hope to sort out the frauds, sham artists and other charlatans from genuine analysis.

An example that is trotted out once a year is the so-called Super Bowl Indicator. Hopefully no one takes it seriously but I fear some may not be in on the joke. For those who have not heard of it this indicator says that if a team from the old NFL (before the merger of the NFL and AFL) wins the Super Bowl then the stock market will be up in the next year. And if an old AFL team wins then the market will be down for the year. What is interesting is that the record shows an amazing 85% or so accuracy in forecasting the market for the year.

Of course it is all baloney and every serious investor merely has a good chuckle over it. I think, however, that there is something very important to be learned from the

Super Bowl Indicator. No, not how to invest for the coming year. Rather, how not to be mislead by seemingly valid indicators. Many are not this obviously silly.

Anyone who has studied formal logic will recognized the fallacy in the Super Bowl Indicator. The fallacy is that simply because A does the same thing B does time after time does not mean that A and B are in any way related. This is sometimes called the Gambler's Fallacy or the Monte Carlo Fallacy. Those names come from the fallacy that infects some gamblers who feel that because the flip of a coin has come up heads 9 times in a row that the "odds" favor the next flip coming up tails. In fact the odds are the same each time the coin is flipped, even if the coin has come up heads 99 times in a row. This assumes, of course, that the coin is equally weighted on each side of the coin, one lopsided coin in weight would tend to favor heads or tails. But that is rare. So too with the Super Bowl Indicator. Even with its 85% "accuracy" there is no obvious relationship to the market. Before leaving it I might say there could be a reason for this accuracy having nothing to do with football. It is the fact that the old NFL teams were generally stronger than the old AFL teams and therefore tended to win more often. Because the stock market over time has tended to go up two years for every one down year combining these facts it is perhaps not too surprising that an old NFL team victory has good odds of producing an up year and by chance alone an AFL team victory might coincide with a down year. But it has no predictive ability as anyone with common sense will see immediately.

Unfortunately you will not always find it so easy to discredit other indicators that claim to predict stock market behavior. Stock market players have identified numerous data series that they are convinced correlate with the stock market. Indeed some of these are quite supportable and useful. Earlier we looked at the "Value Line" annual formula for determining the value of the DJIA based on earnings, dividends and interest rates. Unfortunately you need to study both statistics and formal logic if you want to sort through what is valid and what is not. Statistics so that you will know what data has statistical validity (put in laymen's terms what you can rely on to predict the next market move) and what data lacks validity. Formal logic so you can spot fallacious arguments, arguments that abound in stock market lore.

So the next time you feel like putting real money on the table simply because a particular chart squiggles in a way that a guru claims is significant, or when your favorite indicator of the market flashes a buy or sell signal, just remember the Super Bowl Indicator. Before you commit real money be sure that the indicator has validity statistically and is logically supported. Otherwise put your charts aside and pull out a quarter, give it a flip and let lady luck be your guide!

CHAPTER 4. STOCK MARKET 301 – MARKET TIMING

4.1 BUY AND HOLD

In my early days of investing I acquired a large volume of reading material. Little of that material has survived to be of use today. One little pamphlet I still refer to and find of help. Written by "Barrons" magazine as a teaser piece to entice new subscribers it lists ten basic rules to follow in investing.

Essentially the Barrons rules advise diversifying your investments into several companies and industries. Pruning your investments by selling the worst performing stock, no matter your purchase price, each year. Owning some low yielding stocks to take advantage of capital gains is another recommendation. Finally, and somewhat self serving , to read one investment publication on a regular basis.

While I have gone far beyond the Barron's rules in my own investing, I still find their common sense rules worth reviewing. Just as authors read and reread the 1919 book "Elements of Style" by Strunk and White on a regular basis, to hone their grammar and writing skills, so too the investor should occasionally go back to the fundamentals of investing.

Essentially the Barron's piece counsel a buy and hold philosophy. Pick good stocks in good industries and hold them, pruning out the worst each year.

Many mutual fund companies send out pamphlets to their investors counseling them to buy and hold. They cite numerous examples of successful investment strategy from buying the best investments and holding them. Of course they have a small degree of self interest! However, for many investors they do them a great service. Unless an investor is willing to study market timing and then apply the timing strategy with an unemotional skill then that investor is better off buying and holding.

On the other hand, for those who are willing to learn the basics of market timing they can potentially enhance their overall investment return handsomely and perhaps do so with less risk and less emotional stress in down markets.

In the next section we will discuss various market timing techniques. In this section we will cover the merits of simply buying and holding as an alternative strategy.

The pluses to buying and holding are simple. First, you will never miss the start of an up market. Of course you will not miss the down market either. But, since the long term trend of the market is up you will likely end up ahead in the market over the long term by buying and holding. Particularly if you are buying and holding a well diversified mutual fund or group of funds or a well diversified group of stocks. Second, you will not have to go through the emotional roller coaster of making decisions when to get in and when to get out. Unless you are very skilled at these moves you are likely to get in too late and get out too late. The only thing worse than no timing strategy is to have a bad timing strategy.

Now for the minus. One of the easiest things to do is to fall in love with a stock or mutual fund. The danger of buying and holding is that you will hold long past the time to sell. There comes a time for every stock and for every mutual fund that the wise investor will change to another investment vehicle. The Barron's rules above try to help by counseling you to weed out your stocks each year. Another example is where you own a balance of various mutual funds or stocks to "rebalance" your portfolio at least once a year. Particularly if held in tax advantaged vehicles like an IRA or 401(k). But following the sell once a year or even the rebalancing can be emotionally difficult for the buy and hold investor. It is so easy to rationalize holding on to ATT or IBM or Fidelity Magellan through a period of bad performance.

Another minus is the fact that even mediocre timing of your portfolio to take into account predictable moves in the economy or market can greatly increase your performance. In the sections to follow we will see examples of where timing can greatly increase the return after taxes and after inflation. And since it is so hard to achieve a reasonable return after taxes and inflation any technique that can help your performance is worthy of your careful attention.

If you decide to follow the buy and hold strategy then be sure that you also adopt a rigid rebalancing and weeding out strategy. You must have a way of weeding out the underperforming stocks or mutual funds. Otherwise you are likely to fail in achieving what you want from your investments.

The choice is yours – market time or market weed! Either can work. But you must do one or the other to be a successful investor.

4.2 TIMING STRATEGIES

Market timing strategies come in two forms. First is a strategy based on the business and political cycles. Under this strategy as the economy booms the objective is to move to the sideline near the stop and stay on the sideline until the recession brings the market down. Then you would begin your reentry. There are numerous variations on the theme including industries to be in during early, middle and late stages of a recovery or a recession but for busy people this is far too complicated a strategy. The second strategy is based on moves in the stock market without regard to the underlying economy. This second form may have aspects that take the economy into account but the buy and sell signals it gives pay no attention to the business cycle.

Each of these strategies has merit. Each also has one or more defects. The biggest defect of both systems is that if you are wrong or you let your emotions override a "call" then you stand to be worse off financially than if you bought and held through good times and bad. So before you apply market timing be sure that you are psychologically, financially and intellectually ready. It is nothing to be ashamed about not to be able to market time successfully. Many a pro cannot do it. It is a bit like retailing. In retailing there are super merchants often called Merchant Princes. They are the super stars that always seem to be a jump ahead of what the buying public wants. J.C. Penny, Sam Walton, Fred Lazarus, Jr all had this magic touch. So too the Market Timing Princes. There are some that are outstanding. The problem is that they may be outstanding for years and then have a dry spell. What worked in the last ten years may have run its course.

There are numerous services that offer market timing strategies. Some of these have hotlines and on line services that will give you a minute by minute view of the market. These are services for traders not investors. Other services use no load mutual funds and switch between stocks, bonds and cash or with some variation.

Before we go further I will tell you how I use market timing. I never buy or sell simply on a timing system or because one line crosses another (which is what is mostly involved here). Rather, I use these to help me to buy or sell once I have already made the decision to buy or sell based on where I believe the market is headed for its next major move. For example, let's say I think we are in the late stages of a bull market and that the market is more likely to go down over the next 2 years than it is to go up. I would use market timing to get some (not all) money out of the market and move to more conservative investments. Likewise once I have decided the market is a good value and ripe for an upturn into a new bull market period I use market timing to make my purchases.

Most market timing services will tell you that they can call the turn in the market but not where the market will go. That is useful, but not very. My own analysis helps me pinpoint not only turning points but the likely extent of the move and its duration. I am getting a little ahead of myself but let me explain just a bit to show how market timing and technical analysis helps in making decisions.

My basic market decisions are based on hard economic facts like changes in demographics, changes in technology, movements of population and key economic and monetary factors. My timing decisions are based on letting the market tell me when the other factors I have spotted are beginning to turn the market one direction or another.

By studying past turning points I have noted that stock prices tend to move up or down in lines that parallel each other for specific periods. For example, after a period of down market the upturn tends to continue for 6 to 12 months and move up about 25% on the DJIA or SP500 during this period.

Down moves are trickier. They tend to have periods of disbelief (that the up move is over) and rallies that the pros call bull traps because they make the bulls think the decline is over. The decline generally moves on fairly predictable lines and the market tends to decline on a line about half the angle of the previous uptrend line. This decline goes for 9 to 18 months in most cases. Note I am not talking about major market breaks caused by internal market problems like happened in 1987 with a failure of program trading or in 2010-11 with the flash crashes but rather I am talking about normal market up and down trends. As with Black Swan events (unpredictable events) problems with the market mechanisms can be sharp and severe and they are also unpredictable. When they happen they can offer good entry points for sideline cash but all an investor can do is know they could happen any time and to have sufficient cash reserves to protect themselves in the event sudden and unexpected drops occur.

When we begin to study the methods that I employ you will see that I draw a bright line on the chart based on the long term trend of the markets running back to the 1870's and confirmed by the 1920 to date trend line. Next I identify bold up and down moves and have specific up trend and down trend lines that I look for. In later chapters we will look at charts but for now I want you to focus not on charts but on the concept of timing.

What these lines do for me is to give me a polestar to follow. If I believe that the market's next move is up I will be looking to buy at a point when the timing signals tell me that such a move is in progress. To some extent this is a trend following system but not really. I want to be in before the trend followers or momentum investors get on board. Too much of a major move is lost waiting for the trend to be proven statistically.

An example from the recent past occurred when the first Gulf War was over. After being in sell territory above its long term price line before the war the market moved to an equally pessimistic level below the price line. Not that such a move was unwarranted. Until the war started it was anybody's guess just how bad it could be. Predicting and betting on the outcome that occurred took a true gambler not an investor. However, once the outcome was clear, as it was within 48 hours after Desert Storm commenced, then the investor could have made a move. Movement in the markets made clear very early that the market was ready to move up strongly. Because the down move was so sharp the up move was equally sharp.

This is something to remember. Like a bouncing ball the energy expended in sharp up or down moves generally results in equally sharp counter moves when the primary move ends. October 1987 was one example and January 1991 another and more recently the up move starting in March 2009 still another.

Now that we have seen a little bit of how market timing can work let's look more at the two basic forms of market timing. To distinguish these I will call the first form "Economy Timing" and the second form "Stock Timing." Of course we are timing buys and sells in the stock market in both cases. But in Economy Timing we are looking at fundamental and monetary factors that affect the general economy and therefore affecting they key components of stock value – earnings, dividends and interest rates. With Stock Timing while these factors may be included or may affect the reason the timing system works as it does the chief focus is strictly on the movement of stock prices.

Economy timing is the trickier of the two. Spotting a recession or recovery before the rest of the investment world spots it is indeed tricky. While changes in the economy are clear looking back at them looking forward is like staring into a foggy night.

Fortunately there is a very good service that has an excellent track record for predicting turns in the economy. ECRI, or Economic Cycle Research Institute, grew out of the pioneering work of the econometrician Geoffrey Moore whose work is continued now by the NBER (National Bureau of Economic Research) which is the official arbiter of start and end of recession. Mentioned earlier is a book, "Beating the Business Cycle" which describes what they do in terms anyone can understand. It is well worth reading. But for up to date information once a week at 10:30 eastern time on their website they update their US Indexes and include what they term a "Dashboard" which shows graphically the state of the business cycle both in terms of leading indicators of growth and the prospects for inflation. For a detailed description it is best to refer to their book which will help understand what this all means.

Currently they do not charge for access weekly to these indexes. Their professional service they do charge for but for the average investor using their website weekly or even monthly to check on trends is sufficient. To find this you go to their website www.businesscycle.com and currently at the top there is a heading "Reports and Indexes." If you click on this you will get to the dashboard showing both graphically and numerically where the key components stand as of their release dates. If you click on one of the items in the drop down box you will NOT currently get to the dashboard. As with all websites these change over time so you may have to hunt to find this if they have changed their current site. You will also find here their leading indicator of house prices which for home owners can be helpful in seeing the state of home prices in real (after inflation) terms. This was useful during the housing boom and again in the crash that followed for those trying to time sales or purchases of houses. Unfortunately they no longer provide the chart of this in their free service.

There are many other services that provide timing information on the economy but I have found that ECRI is the most useful of all of them. It has a very good track record during the more than ten years I have followed them. One caution, they may be right about the economy but it may or may not translate into movements in stocks. For example in 2013 with interest rates at zero for four years and the Federal Reserve expecting this to continue in to 2015 despite weakness in the overall economy (slow growth if not recession) predicted by ECRI the stock market has continued strong as its performance and dividends have provided a competitive environment compared to money market, CD or bond yields. This is clearly an aberration but how long it will continue is anyone's guess.

Later I will be discussing a quarterly chart of the SP500index and various stock market tools that I believe are helpful in deciding when markets may turn down or up. In making my decision I use ECRI data to determine if what the Stock Timing signals are showing me are consistent with the underlying economic trends. Just as I use the annual

Value Line chart to give me a polestar of what earnings, dividends and interest rates show about the current and possible future values of this index.

I also use Economic Timing more for getting into the market than getting out. As with most investors I find that as a bull market and a growth period extend into the 4th year and beyond I am looking for an eventual decline. But there is no economic reason a growth period cannot extend 8 or 10 years ore more. Especially as we move into the post industrial period the old regularity of the business cycle becomes questionable. As we will discuss in a later chapter I fear that potential downturns in the post industrial period could be more savage than in the industrial period and recoveries more tepid. Unlike the V shaped decline and recovery of industrial recessions we are finding post industrial recessions can result in sharp declines but slow recoveries (alas there is no letter in the alphabet to describe this).

Once a recession commences I am reasonably comfortable in thinking that two years is probably the outside and nine to eighteen months is more likely to be the duration of the recession. Therefore six months into a recession (about the time it is called a recession since there is always a reality lag in spotting the decline) I begin to look for the up move. Here I use Economy Timing to help. I look at such factors as monetary conditions, cuts in the discount rate, status of business inventories and the rate at which corporate insiders are buying the stocks of cyclical companies in the open market as opposed to exercising stock options. But it is ECRI on which I rely the most watching for them to call the turn. In this they have been excellent over the last ten years. Favorable developments in these factors makes me start looking at the Stock Timing factors to decide when to redeploy cash into stocks.

During a recession, especially the last one, interest rates on money market and CD's declined and have been close to zero now for over four years. Holding cash is painful in those times but putting it to work and suffering capital losses is even worse. So you need to steel yourself emotionally not to move back into stocks too soon in these conditions. It is not easy to do, knowing you are losing to inflation and taxes holding cash at zero or low interest rates, but the alternative can be even worse.

Stock Timing has an incredible number of systems. Even to try and summarize the major ones would take a book in itself.

Most of the Stock Timing systems rely on letting the market itself tell you what is happening. They look mainly at moving averages of stock prices, whether or not volume of stock trading is increasing and a host of other factors.

The simplest systems are moving averages. To develop a moving average you start with an average. Let's say you want to watch the DJIA and you want to use a 20 day moving average. First you collect the last 20 day closing prices, add them up and divide by 20. Now you have an average. As each trading day passes you take the number you divided by 20 and add the current day's close and subtract the close on the day 21 days in the past. This leaves you with a total for 20 days including the present day. Then you divide by 20 and now you have a moving average. Most people plot these on a graph with the DJIA plotted on the same graph. If you do this over time you will see the DJIA moves on both sides of its 20 day average. If I am getting ready to buy or sell I will look how far above or below the 20 day average the DJIA is selling. When I find that it is at a low level relative to its average for the past several months and if I am planning to buy then this may be a good time. Likewise if I want to sell and the DJIA is selling substantially above its average I may use that time to sell. As you will see if you do this charting the DJIA will stay above its average for long periods of time and below its average for long periods. All this tells you is a little something about the momentum of the market. Later we will see the techniques I suggest you consider and it will include these averages computed for you.

Another factor that the professionals use is momentum. They have developed an amazing number of technical indicators using momentum. Most of these are helpful but are beyond the normal use by those whose business is not the markets. I tend to use fairly simple systems I have found helpful. For example, after a fairly dull period in the market if the market moves up on a high volume day I find that for the next several days the momentum in the market is usually up. Again, I never use these techniques to sell or buy unless my fundamental analysis tells me it is a time to make a move.

A number of mutual fund switch strategies are based on moving averages. Usually a 200 day moving average. When the market moves through its 200 day moving average on the upside most of these services will flash a buy signal. Likewise when the 200 day moving average is crossed on the downside they will flash a sell signal.

These systems have the virtue of simplicity. The problem with them is in a trendless market. A market where the prices of stocks move up and down in a range of 200 points or so. The investor following the switch systems in such a time can be nibbled to death. Financially that is. Buying and selling, or switching from stock to cash on a frequent basis often results in more losses than gains. In a major trend market, up or down, these systems work extremely well. Some of them have tried to build in various techniques that avoid the whipsawing of a trendless market.

For the busy investor it is unlikely you will use these techniques other than a couple that I will discuss below. But it is helpful to know about them as you will run across them from time to time. The ultimate objective of this book is not to teach you all the tricks of the trade but to cover them broadly so you will have some basic knowledge. In all likelihood you will not want to fool with these but instead put together a diversified portfolio of stocks that do not require your day to day management.

4.3 STOP LOSS STRATEGIES

The idea of a stop loss is to fix a price at which you want to be out of a stock. If you buy a stock at $50 thinking it will go to $100 you might put a stop loss at $45 or a 10% loss. Then as the price goes up (hopefully) you might move your stop loss up so as to protect a part of your profit. If the stock goes to $75 for example and you are staying with a 10% stop loss you would set the stop loss at $75-7.5 = $67.50.

Most believers in stop loss are trying to get investors to take emotion out of the market by fixing their exit points. The stop loss can be a true stop loss; that is an order to your broker to sell at a fixed price. Or you can set a mental stop loss. If you are working with a mutual fund or you want to be out of the market, in whole or in part, at a fixed price in an average then you will have to set a mental stop and act on it yourself rather than rely on the automatic stop loss with your broker. Stop losses do not work with mutual funds, other than a special subset of ETF or closed end mutual funds (about which more later).

Several very good analysts believe in stop losses. Marty Zweig was one of these. In his investment service continued after his passing Zweig sets stop losses for every order that he places. His theory is that since he is a trend follower he is willing to give up part of his gains to follow the trend as far as it will go. But, he does not want to get caught in the euphoria of the moment and fail to sell when the trend is clearly changing.

There are several problems with stop losses. First they are hard to set, especially in the day of hedge fund trading where markets can gyrate wildly without indicating a change in the trend. If you set the stop loss too close to the market you will find yourself sold out on a blip to the downside. If you set it too far away to protect against momentary blips then you may suffer a good size loss. Finally there are technical problems with a broker stop loss. Most people think they will be sold out when the prices reaches their stop loss. In most cases this will be true but on big market declines, such as the crash in 1987, or several minicrashes since then, the price may fall through your stop loss and you will be stopped out at much lower prices than you thought.

All this having been said there are times that I like to use stop losses. First, I always have mental stop losses set based on my trend lines and my overall view of the market and the economy supporting it. Usually these are based on the Dow or S&P averages but I set other stops for particular mutual funds or stocks. I don't always follow these stops. For example, my stops were triggered in 1990 but I elected not to act on them. In retrospect I would have been wiser to have followed my stops but the market did eventually recover as I anticipated. What I did not anticipate was the valley in between! On the other hand I did act on my stops in 1987, the day before the big crash on Black Monday. I had set a mental stop loss that was triggered on Friday before the crash. True, I had lost out on a couple of hundred DJIA points from the top, but I was still substantially ahead for the year and father ahead than I would have been without these mental stops --- and acting on them.

At the present time I stay pretty close to the markets and can act quickly if need be. At other times in my career I did not have that luxury. During those times I used either actual stop losses or mental stop losses. My personal feeling about stop losses is that on the whole, like buying on margin or short selling (both bad ideas for the average or even above average investor) they should not be used by most investors. If you have the right temperament to be in the markets you should develop early the decisiveness needed to get in (when everyone else is getting out) and to get out (when everyone else is getting in) and to put emotion behind you. Since I am just as human as the next person I use my own emotions as a partial judge. Whenever I "feel" I should be getting out I sit back and take a look at whether I really should be getting in (if out) or investing more (if in already). Also, when I feel like I should jump on the bandwagon, that I am being left behind if I do not invest even more then that is when I sit back and think perhaps it is a time to head for the exit. When I have these "feelings" it is usually because through the press, commentators, etc. I am feeling like most people in the market.

Real money is often made by going against the crowd, not with it. On the other hand I know from history that trends, be they up or down, tend to go much further than people think. So when I have these feelings I tend to set stop losses (or if I am then out the market I set reentry points) near the current market and at which point I would be happy with the profits that I would take were I to be stopped out or if I am reentering then at a price I would be happy with even if the market goes down further. Since I set these mentally I can adjust them if the move is based on program trading or some other gyration that I feel is not a genuine change of trend. Of course that subjects me to second guessing my own stop losses. But I would prefer to make a mistake or two second guessing than to have a rigid system that acts thoughtlessly. To take a recent example from housing I am sure all remember how many times people were "certain" housing would continue to go up and you just had to buy a house, or more house, as an investment. Likewise once the bust came no one wanted to touch housing. Guess who made the most money in housing? Those that sold when everyone was convinced housing prices could never go down and those that bought when no one wanted to buy again. The same is true in the stock market.

Before we leave stop losses there is one final aspect to consider and that is taxes. Unfortunately the current tax system severely penalizes savers and investors. We are still living in the Keynesian era that worships at the shrine of spending and with only grudgingly acknowledges the role of saving and investment.

Most investment advisers tell you to ignore the tax effects of your investment decisions. They are right. . . and they are wrong. They are right that you should not let tax considerations alone make your decision, if it is time to sell you should sell, even if that means higher taxes. Well, maybe.

If you are an 80 year old in poor health with substantial assets you want to pass on to your heirs with major capital gains that would be currently taxed but which would be forgiven (stepped up in basis in tax language) you will consider whether or not to sell differently than a 20 year old in a low tax bracket.

The point is that you should take taxes into account in your investing and the tax effect of a particular decision to sell should be a factor in your decision. It should not be the only factor. Many an investor has had a gain they sought to protect from taxes, only to later sell at a loss instead of a gain. There can be no hard and fast rules here. But using stop losses to try and gain short term market advantages needs to be weighed against the transaction and tax costs of the move. Of course in tax advantaged accounts like 401(k) and IRA's there are no immediate tax effects of selling. But in taxable accounts you may be better riding through a valley in the market if you see one coming than to subject yourself to the market and tax risks of moving in and out of the market.

One exception to considering taxes is if you have a loss in a taxable account and want to lock in that loss for tax purposes before the end of the tax year. At present you can offset gains with losses and use up to $3000 a year against ordinary income. In addition loss you cannot use this year will carry forward to future years. But remember there is what is called a Wash Sale. That is if you buy the same security less than 31 days before or after the date of the security sale the same security your loss will be washed out and you cannot use it until the purchased securities are sold. The rule on profits is different. You can sell one minute and buy the next and gains are taxable. Or you can buy an essentially equivalent investment e.g., selling one mutual fund and buying one that has a similar strategy at the same time. Of course there is no guarantee those securities will act the same. Then after 31 days you can go back to the original fund if you want. This book is not intended to give you more than thumbnail idea about taxes and since tax rules change frequently if you plan to consider taxes in your investment plan you need to know the current rules.

4.4 MARKET CYCLES

Probably more is written about market cycles than most other market subjects. Something fascinates us about cycles. Maybe it is all the cycles in nature that makes cycles have a special fascination for us. After all we have cycles of the moon, seasons, weather and a host of other natural phenomena.

The danger in cyclical analysis is that it is like the Super Bowl Indicator. It gives the appearance of exactitude. Every day you watch one of the financial channels or read a financial publication like the Wall Street Journal or Investor's Business Daily and some pundit will be pronouncing that at exactly 3 PM on a date certain the market will turn up or down based on a cycle that they have identified. The hardest part of cycle interpretation is just that, "interpretation." One of the crazes is the Elliot Wave Analysis. The theory predicts certain specific behavior waves of price movements of stocks and of whole markets. The problem is that, like astrologers, these predictors of the future tend to disagree with each other in where the waves start and stop. As a result at any one time you can find them wildly disagreeing on where we are or where we are going.

I am reminded of when I was a young attorney in the Air Force and exposed to my first real life lie detector application. At the time polygraphs had been banned in criminal investigation in the Air Force (for good reason I might add) unless requested by the subject under investigation. My client was so strenuous in his defense that we decided to risk the giving of a lie detector to him. As I learned more and more about the process I had less and less confidence in what was going on. Not that the Air Force was acting improperly, to the contrary they were scrupulous in what they did and above board in their actions. I began to become uneasy about the process when I was told that they could not show me on the tape where a subject was lying or telling the truth. This was a matter of "interpretation" by the operator. Hmmmm. Looked like tea leaf reading to me. Then under the Baxter method (then the recognized standard) I was told that the incriminating question was surrounded by questions that were accusatory but clearly innocent. If the subject reacted less to the guilty question than the innocent question that indicated innocence. If he reacted just the same to all three questions the results were inconclusive. And if he reacted more to the guilty question than the innocent questions then he was lying. Good Grief! Who in the world would not react more to a question that they knew was important than to one that they knew was irrelevant? I soon realized what the lie detector was really used for. By a skilled defense attorney, having access to his own preferred operator he can test his client and profess just how innocent he is. To the authorities the test can result in a finding that the subject is lying. . . at which point many a subject will see the light and come clean. And there is one place on the tape they can show you deception and it is used to convince you these modern astrologers really can read your mind. You pick a number from 1 to 10 and when asked each number in turn you say "no" when asked if that is your number. Then the operator tells you the number you picked. Thinking about this it is relatively easy to see how this can work but where it is much more speculative when used in a complex question about guilt or innocence.

There are many people that believe in the efficacy of polygraphs but I am not among them. I wish that it were really that easy. I know now why the courts refuse to give them credence. Yet there are many who swear by them almost with religious fervor. Those inexperienced with the method can be understandably forgiven if they feel that the experts must know what they are doing. After all the equipment looks so impressive and in a 1 to 10 number sequence they can actually show the effectiveness.

So what is the point? The point is that many cycle interpreters are on as shaky a logical and scientific foundation as the polygraph operators are. And yet they can be equally impressive.

Next time you are inclined to put money on the table (or take it off the table) based on a cyclical theory or the squiggling line of some indicator, remember the polygraph and the Super Bowl Indicator. That does not mean that you ignore cycles or indicators, merely that you do not give them significance beyond what they deserve.

A. GENERATIONAL/ KONDRATIEFF CYCLES

Kondratieff was a Russian economist who felt that he had identified a long (58 year) cycle in the behavior of capitalist societies. For the last 50 years there are many who have been looking for the dreaded down turn in the Kondratieff Wave. Virtually all of these feel that the last downdraft started in 1929-32 with the Great Depression. It does not take much of a math student to see that the next down wave would have occurred in the 1987-90 time period. One reason the 1987 market crash, the first over 20% decline in a day since the Great Depression crash of 1929, was so scary to people. Any wonder that some thought the world was truly ending with the 1987 crash.

Then there is Dr. Batra who called for a Great Depression beginning in 1990. He sold a lot of books based on this theory. While he did not rely on Kondratieff I doubt the Russian was totally out of his mind when the prediction was made. Now I may be reading my words a few years from now and eating them but I think that the Kondratieff bottom came in the middle 1970's when we had a depression that affected stock prices and other values for over 15 years. I will admit that many of the underpinnings of the Kondratieff Wave still appear to be a problem, excessive debt and speculation for example, and inflation may be coming back into the economy. These are the types of excesses that Kondratieff felt afflicted every other generation in capitalistic societies- where excesses tend to build until they are unwound only with a great collapse of economic activity. Just like we are seeing in housing at the present time in 2007-2013. From the ashes of that collapse arises a new phoenix of economic activity. It would appear that perhaps the next period for collapse could come in 2032 which just happens to coincide with the worst effects of the Baby Boom generation peaking in economic cost.

By analyzing the Kondratieff Wave I do not want to give the impression that I agree with it. There is simply in my mind insufficient hard scientific proof that would satisfy a statistician that there is valid evidence supporting his theory. On the other hand I do think there tend to be generational cycles that occur and bear some attention.

I do believe that generations often must learn the hard way the lessons that they should learn from the history of prior generations. There is something in human beings that makes us feel that we are wiser than our parents, that the history they lived through is no longer relevant and that this time it will be different. Perhaps that is just as well. Give each new generation a clean slate on which to write, spelling errors and all. Maybe the burden of history is just too great to bear and man can only move forward if that burden is left by the side of the road. True, as the great philosopher Santayana has told us, "those who ignore the past are doomed to repeat it." Yet, maybe there is a corollary to this saying...those who dwell too much on the past may fall into the next hole in the road while looking back at the old one. Probably a germ of truth in each.

Economic history does show patterns that tend to repeat themselves. Patterns that do seem to have some support from enduring tendencies in human nature both individually and collectively, in the form of businesses or governments. For example it is a rare government that is able to print money and at the same time resist the urge to print more of the stuff when the need arises and they find their expenses outrunning their income. Those are the modern heirs to the traditions of the Roman emperors who clipped the coinage and debased it to hide a tax increase. The current gold bug is not that far removed from the citizen of Rome who knew that to trust the currency was a prescription for disaster.

On a smaller scale history is replete with manias (a special form of cyclical behavior) that have separated various fools from their money. Are baseball playing cards that far removed from tulips? Not really. One of the truly great books to read before investing is "Extraordinary Popular Delusions and the Madness of Crowds." Written by Charles Mackay over 200 years ago it analyzes various forms of crowd madness that has afflicted society from time to time with various forms of mental plague. From witch hunting to the South Sea Bubble and my (and most economist's) personal favorite, the Dutch tulip mania. Mankind has repeatedly been led astray by the false illusion of quick profit or fear of the unknown. Recent collapse of the internet stock bubble and housing bubble are only modern manifestations of these manias.

In the middle of the 16th Century the Dutch tulip mania occurred and it is worth special mention. The Dutch became convinced that tulip bulbs had a special value and the bulbs were bid higher and higher, to absurd prices. Of course the higher they went the higher everyone was convinced they would go. As the early tulip collectors cashed in their profits those who first thought the whole thing foolish began to think that they missed out on something good. Then, as with all manias, one day some one woke up and realized that all they had were tulip bulbs, and the whole thing collapsed.

While baseball cards have yet to reach the mania stage prices of impressionist painters, collectible Ferrari automobiles and real estate prices of the first decade of this Century we have seen prices rise in many markets to absurd levels only to later collapse.

Cycles exist because there are certain patterns in nature and in human nature that tend to repeat themselves. If you can identify true cycles from false cycles you can profit greatly from them. But beware overreliance lest you are left holding the tulip bulb when the music stops (to mix my metaphors).

Without either crediting or discrediting Kondratieff, I do believe that they are generational cycles where greed and fear alternate. Where one time the sky is the limit and the next the sky is falling. Where debts are accumulating to the breaking point much like the first rise of a roller coaster and then the peak is reached and you plunge downward in a stomach wrenching decline. While this leads me to agree with the principles of cycles I am less in agreement that the timing of cycles can be accurately predicted. So for the thoughtful economist/investor I am urging study of cycles but also urging extreme care in thinking them exact.

Now for my own thoughts on the current conditions looking back over some 100 plus years of investment in the United States.

After the depression of the 1930's and WWII there began a long recovery and movement steadily upward through the middle of the 1960's. Then we had a period of 16 years of stagnation where stock prices declined in terms of buying power. Only in 1975 did this trend reverse and real improvement occurred only in the early 1980's. Even now, we have scarcely recovered sufficiently to put stock prices on an upward path once inflation is removed.

It seems to me that these up trends, once established, have tended to last 25 years or so (remember that it is dangerous to rely on exact numbers when investing) followed by a period of about 15 years of decline. This is a 40 year time frame, different from the Kondratieff Wave, but not that dissimilar in analysis.

As the economy steadily moves higher and higher more and more risks are taken that would not have been taken after the end of the last decline. The latest of these was the high risk syndication of mortgages but it is not the first and will certainly not be the last time greed overcomes judgment. In the book I wrote in 1990 I said that the next major turning point would likely come around 2007. Turns out that was almost exactly correct. No magic there, however. Also no exactness since I said it could be as early as 2000 or late as 2015. Well, I am one to hedge just a bit! Whenever we are in an upturn more and more people will come up with more and more reasons why the trend will go up forever....this time! Be it Y2K and the internet bubble or the housing boom that followed.

The economic analysis supporting this thesis is as follows. The problems that we had in the 1970's were two fold. For 25 years we had the benefit of a world economy recovering from war and depression. The United States was the primary engine of that growth. But by 1975 the rebuilt economies of Japan and Germany found themselves with the latest equipment, technology, and markets and they became exporters in a big way, competing with U.S. industry that had aging equipment, old technology, and older markets. At the same time in the U.S. the labor force was having to absorb the Baby Boom that followed WWII. It was a time, unusual in modern history, when man began to replace machine. Why automate fast food restaurants when there were hoards of kids ready and eager to work? This meant a decline in productivity, since most gains in productivity are not the result of harder or smarter work but of machines that can produce more, faster. Pressure on wages abated with so much labor available. True there were shortages in certain skills but not in the overall labor force. Finally, to try and keep up on the economic treadmill more and more women entered the labor force. A trend starting after WWI and accelerating after WWII. Whether the women's movement was a cause of or caused by this trend we will probably never know for certain. The militancy of women pushing into the work force added even more pressure. As with most resources, the more there are the cheaper they are. The result of all this was that the distribution to the whole labor force was no greater than before, the pie was simply cut more ways.

The alienation that this brought, along with the absence of parents at home in my mind has helped to create a large part of the current social problems from undereducated children to drugs. But my purpose here is economic, not political or social, and the economic effect of all this was one of stagnation, inflation with low growth rates in what came to be called "stagflation."

Back in 1990 I stated my view that this should change by the middle 1990's when there would be shortages of labor, more replacement of men by machines, more productivity. And this is exactly what happened with the computer and the internet making major gains in productivity possible. With the dramatic changes in Eastern Europe I thought that we would find entire new markets opening up that would give all of the industrial democracies whole new markets and opportunities that would raise living standards of both the old and the new democracies. I then stated that I thought if all this comes to pass then the rest of the millennium and first few years of the 21st Century would be very good and indeed they were.

Now for the bad news. Beginning in 2007 or so the Baby Boom began to retire. At least I thought they would want to retire. Just as their entry into the labor force caused problems, their exit will cause even more problems. Pressures on social security, medical facilities, etc. all will increase. And the younger generation will likely feel increasingly burdened by the older.

At the same time the development of the new democracies in Eastern Europe should result in their being in the position of Japan and Germany in the 1970's. They will become net exporters and competitors with those who helped them develop. Well, that has not really come to pass and I did not foresee the symbiotic relationship that has developed with India and China providing cheap out sourced labor for developed economy industries. Ok, so I am not perfect in my prognostications!

At the time I did predict another period of stagnation, be it depression or stagflation and if the estimate of 15 years (plus or minus) proves accurate then the next up leg in terms of a "real" stock market advance may not occur until 2022 to 2025. Now 21 plus years after making that prediction I see no reason to change it.

All of which is vitally important to the long term investor. The long term investor wants to ride the up wave as long a possible and then seek to protect themselves during the stagnation decline. Very easy to say…very difficult to implement.

Whether or not there is validity to the generational cycle, it is worth paying attention to. I said in 1990 the following…."If I am around in 2007, I will be watching very carefully what is happening and will hopefully be setting my exit points for my stock investments to ease the pain of the bad years. During those years I will be studying which of the two likely scenarios will play out – a depression like the 1930's, stagflation like the 1970's or maybe a third possibility, hyperinflation followed by a collapse similar to Germany after WWI." Now in 2013 I can say that I followed my own advice but unfortunately the story is not yet at an end and sadly the third possibility is still very much on the table and the next five to ten years will reveal which of these possibilities comes to pass. This is one prediction I would be very, very happy to find is wrong! So far the stagflation scenario seems to be the one playing out but we are still in the early innings of this ballgame.

Unfortunately the investment actions one should take are different depending which of the three scenarios comes to pass. As with human disease, proper diagnosis and quick treatment is necessary to avoid great suffering. At least this generational analysis may be helpful in mapping out your strategy should you confront these economic conditions.

B PRESIDENTIAL CYCLES

Of all the cycles that affect the stock market the one that I find most credible is the so-called Presidential Election Cycle.

Stated simply the thesis is that Presidents like to be re-elected. Accordingly if they must take economic pain to slow an overheating economy they will do so early in their administration. Then, especially in the first term of a new President, they will do everything possible to pump up the economy in time for their re-election. Once the election is over they will slam on the brakes to stop the excesses they created to ensure their election. Then the cycle repeats. The theory and analysis is much more sophisticated but this is the essence.

For investors, the idea is to be in the market more heavily after the off year Congressional elections and lighten up after the Presidential election. As with most things cyclical there are exceptions and while the concept works it has had some failures. Nevertheless the economic underpinnings of the cycle are valid as are the political/human nature tendencies at work. So, everything else being equal, if you feel that you should step aside from the market and it is around the time of the most recent Presidential election then the turn of the cycle would be one more reason to step aside, lighten up or move to more defensive positions depending on just how dismal you think the situation may be. On the other hand, if you think that the market may be reaching a buying juncture and you are near the off year Congressional elections then this would be another reason to consider moving more into the market increasing your investments or taking a more aggressive stand.

There are a number of books that discuss the Presidential Cycle in detail and if interested do a search for Presidential Cycle to locate them. One of the best is [The Little Book of Stock Market Cycles (Little Books. Big Profits)](#) by Hirsch, Jeffrey A. and Kass, Douglas A. (Jul 9, 2012) but check for more recent editions.

C. BUSINESS CYCLES

That there are cycles in business matters in undeniable. Just how useful they are in predicting the future is something else. And even if they can predict the economy the interrelationship with stocks and other investments may be difficult to find. We study these cycles so we can try to learn from the past in order to better understand the present and the future. Politicians use them to make policy decisions. Business leaders use them to try to predict what will happen to their business. Investors use them to try and predict where stock prices will go or how a business or industry will be affected by what is happening.

The problem with cycle studies is to know when the conditions that made the cycle work as a predictor of the future have changed to make it no long reliable. Unfortunately that is usually known only in hindsight.

Let's take an example or two. Industrial economies have different cycles than agricultural economies. Agricultural economies tend to have cycles that depend on weather conditions and demand for their product that may be affected by demand from an industrial economy. For example, the state of an economy based on cotton production will be affected first by weather in the cotton growing regions along with pests and other blights and by the demand for its product from industrial economies.

Industrial economies tend to have more regular business cycles. Starting from the top of a business cycle as business perceives demand weakening businesses start to cut back on inventory building. This in turn cuts back demand for the producers of raw materials and suppliers of semi finished products to these businesses. They in turn cut back on their buying of product. As the inventories wind down in the system lay off of workers is inevitable. These laid off workers don't spend as they did before and others fearing they may be next start to save for the rainy day they see ahead. Thus total demand for product declines further, inventories may be reduced further and on it goes until the cycle finally exhausts itself and reaches a bottom. When it does then the inventory rebuilding begins and an upswing in demand commences.

This is a very simplified and therefore highly inaccurate version of the industrial business cycle. Obviously much more than inventories and consumer demand are involved. In modern, complex societies the interrelationships are often fuzzy and unclear. Economists use a variety of input/output analyses, econometric modeling and other ways of trying to measure and anticipate moves in the business cycle. While some are better than others, none that I know of are perfect. Coming close is the ECRI leading indicators that will be discussed in some detail below.

All this is by way of background, to caution you about cycles before we look at what they may tell us. Because they make for pretty graphs and accurate looking forecasts there is a tendency to give cycle predictions more credibility than they deserve. Cycle analysis is at best a guesstimate for the future. Used properly it can be quite helpful. They key is to recognize that no matter how accurate a cycle has been in the past that conditions can and do change and a cycle may then lose its effectiveness as a predictor of the future.

For example, throughout the 1980's economists were waiting year after year for a recession that never came. It finally arrived in 1990, many years after it had been predicted. Those who conducted their investments or business affairs based on the forecasters of recession missed out on much of the 1980's up thrust. Recessions are hard to predict. Much harder than moves from a recession. That is another point to ponder. Some cycles as prediction instruments work well in one direction and not in another.

There is an old saw among economists that the index of leading economic indicators published by the National Bureau of Economic Research has predicted nine of the last four recessions. A point always worth remembering about all cycle analysis. As good as cycle analysis is, and some is very good, use it with caution.

One of the problems with business cycle analysis today is that the U.S. and European economies are no longer agricultural or industrial economies. They are post industrial or service oriented and more and more technology dominated. Lest there be any doubt consider the explosive growth and wealth created by E Bay, Google, Apple and Facebook. Seemingly overnight new technological giants can emerge when the fog lifts over Silicon Valley. For example, less than 25% of the United States GDP is currently from the manufacturing part of the economy and fewer than 18% of the jobs are in that sector. And with overseas production and out sourcing the trend is only getting more pronounced. We have truly become a service/technology post industrial economy. The services sector (from fast food to financial institutions to technology services) has grown enormously since WWII, as most economists predicted. Since the 1990's it has accelerated even more. The cycles of a services/information age economy are likely to be as different from an industrial economy as it was different from an agricultural economy.

No one would try to predict what would happen in an industrial economy based on its agricultural component. Yet today many economists still use the tools of the industrial economy to try to predict the future of the service based economy. I believe that is why they generally failed to accurately predict the start of the recession in 1990 and had been looking for that recession since 1985.

We know far too little about the cycles of a post industrial economy to try and make accurate predictions. ECRI has recently predicted that we will see more frequent recessions and recovery from them will be slower than in the past. I suspect they may be right. Unlike industrial companies, service companies rely more on labor and technology and there are very few good gauges of productivity in a service company. Therefore, the tendency is to increase or reduce staffing levels based on very hazy notions of appropriate levels of staffing. The result seems to be that once the problem of over staffing is discovered the amount of over staffing is already immense. Hence massive layoffs result rather than a planned scale back.

Therefore, while it was important in the past to study new orders, inventory to sales levels and similar measure of the state of an industrial economy we have not yet developed similar measures for our post industrial society.

The result is that I am very suspicious about using much of the past cycle work to predict the economic future in the current economy in the Western world. I suspect that when the work is done over the next several decades that we will find a service based economy is much harder to take into recession and is also much harder to bring out of recession. The monetary and fiscal tools that we used so successfully for most of the last century may prove to be dated in dealing with our new economy. The actions of the Federal Reserve after the 2008-09 financial disaster would seem to support this view. And the jury remains out on the effect and effectiveness of what was done in that crisis.

If this is accurate then there are some potentially nasty surprises ahead. Our politicians who have successfully used the Presidential Election Year Cycle to slam on the brakes after the Presidential Election and then floor the accelerator around the time of the mid year Congressional elections may find their timing badly affected.

If this analysis is correct then trying to invest money based on the condition of the business cycle will become far more difficult. Since my hypothesis is that the service/information based societies will tend to build to greater excesses than their industrial ancestors the subsequent redressing of these excesses may also be longer and more painful. It was hard enough to move displaced industrial workers to new jobs. Service and information based workers with narrow skills will possibly be even more difficult to reabsorb. The current downsizing of the financial sector will be interesting to watch to see how these displaced workers are absorbed into the economy.

Having put up my caution flags about using cycles the next section will deal with what cycles can do for the investor.

First, forget cycle analysis to help you pick the top and bottom of the market. Cycles are better used in trying to spot the bottom of the market. Since the market anticipates business conditions it is one of the leading indicators of the general economy. Therefore, once cycles tell us that a downturn is starting or in process it is generally too late to adjust your portfolio.

What is more useful is to spot the bottom. Since the stock market will have already moved down in anticipation of the recession once the business cycles tell you that we are headed down you can look over the valley and look for when the upswing may start. This was much easier when we were in an industrial economy. Once inventories to sales stopped declining and new orders began to level off a move upward was usually only a few months away. Maybe this will still prove true today. But I think that you had better count more on corporate earnings to tell you when the bottom has arrived. When reductions in earnings begin to slow or bottom out and when dividend cuts slow to a trickle then the upturn is probably in sight.

Unlike the rebound that occurred in industrial recoveries we will probably find a much milder rebound off a bottom for a post industrial economy. While industrial cycles tended to be V shaped it is likely that post industrial recoveries will be U shaped. While service companies may be slow to fire in the start of the recession they will likely be also slow to rehire in the recovery. This is good news for inflation and probably long term very good news for stocks and bonds. It is not so good news for those looking for jobs.

Knowing where you are in the business cycle can assist an investor in two ways. First, to be sure you are not fighting against an economic trend. Second, to try and spot updraft and downdraft opportunities or pitfalls in the market.

For example, the most powerful up moves in the stock market generally occur at the end of a recessionary period. Especially when a bear market in stocks has accompanied the recession, as it did in 2007-09. Knowing the signs of the end of the recession can be very helpful in participating in this move. Furthermore, knowing about this potential will enable the nimble investor to jump on the bandwagon relatively early in the trend rehearsal. Use of the ECRI leading indicators discussed in more detail below will give you the edge in anticipating recessions and recoveries. But you need to know early since waiting for the trend to be fully established can cause you to miss out on a large part of the recovery. And always remember that while they may be right about the state of the economy this does not always mean the stock market will behave in a similar manner. Especially if the Federal Reserve is keeping interest rates exceptionally low as it has since 2008. This can distort any cycle pattern.

It is harder to try and predict down turns in the market from analyzing the economy although that is useful. Tops are the hardest to spot. So be aware of cycles but use them mainly to spot the trend of the economy that the market may be following and to spot uptrend potentials at the bottom.

An example of the danger of watching the economy too closely as a guide to investing comes from the late 1940's and early 1950's. In that time period earnings and dividends did not do much and the overall economy looked sluggish. Indeed two recessions occurred in this period and some spikes in inflation. But the stock market roared out of this period, starting a real advance that ended only in the period 1963-73.

As we discussed earlier in looking at the annual Value Line projection for the market, underlying earnings, dividends and interest rates form the sound economic basis for the stock market projections. With these factors known, Value Line's analysis is quite revealing. Their trend line has been remarkably accurate. Unfortunately it is not until after the fact that all of these factors to plug into their equation are known. Therefore as a predicting device the method has real problems. It is still useful but not something to bet your future on. What is useful is the knowledge that these fundamentals have proved to be the rock solid basis of the market. Despite hedge funds, program trading, derivatives and institutional involvement in stocks, the fundamentals still sway the market over the long pull.

Study of business cycles will also help an investor to follow two of the cardinal rules of modern technical investing. First is to never fight the Federal Reserve. The Federal Reserve with its control of the money supply and interest rates has a powerful effect on business and the markets. The rule not to try to fight against the trend of Federal Reserve decisions is a wise one. When the Fed is trying to tighten monetary conditions investors want to be very cautious in the market. It is a time to tighten up mental stop loss positions and change market positions when monetary trend reversals occur. Likewise, when the Fed is loosening the monetary reins and pumping money into the system it is not the time to be short the market or sitting on the sidelines. While the lag time for the Fed can be considerable, favorable monetary conditions are very positive for equity investments.

A second cardinal rule is to "never fight the tape" although with the elimination of ticker tape this does not have the same meaning as before computers! I started my investing days sitting with my grandfather's brother on the balcony of a local hotel where a now defunct brokerage,B.C. Christopher, had a chalk board on which prices were entered and a glass domed ticker tape machine that spit out reams of half inch tape with prices and symbols printed. End of day I had a bushel basket of these to take home. Great fun for a 9 year old. But without ticker tape the concept remains the same. What this means is that when stock prices are trending in a particular direction you will make more money by following rather than fighting this trend. While there are major exceptions at the beginning and end of trends, during the trend itself this is an excellent rule to follow. Again, by knowing the state of the business cycle you will be in a position to judge whether the trend is a solid one (based on economic reality) or whether it is a speculative bubble like the ones before the 1987 crash, the internet bubble an bust of 2000 or the real estate bubble and bust of 2007-9.

It is far beyond the purpose of this book to try and cover the study of business cycles in detail. While useful to an investor they should be only a part of what you watch to make your investment decisions. In a later chapter we will be discussing how to fit this into a plan for your investments so that you do not spend more time than necessary knowing where we are in a cycle.

CHAPTER FIVE ECONOMIC BACKGROUND

5.1 DEMOGRAPHICS AND SCIENTIFIC DEVELOPMENTS

It is important in investing to separate major trends from squiggles up and down that occur. It is something like filtering out the noise that interferes with a TV program you are trying to watch. In the last chapter we discussed one set of filters, using cycles to spot major trends. In this chapter we will look at a different set of filters. These are a bit harder to work with since they are major sociological and scientific changes that can affect your investing.

Again a cautionary note. I have known a lot of investors who have gotten carried away investing on what they saw to be major scientific or social changes. It is easy to read the advanced scientific journals and listen to leading social scientists and get a read on what the next ten to fifty years may look like in terms of new developments. Even if you get that right making money from the changes may be more difficult than you think.

Even if you can spot "growth" industries of the future picking the winning companies can be immensely difficult. A couple of examples. In the 1940's it was obvious that the computer held great promise for the future. What was not so obvious (until much later) was that IBM would be the winning company. Likewise in the 1920's it was obvious that aircraft would be a spectacular market but picking the winning manufacturers and airlines proved much more difficult. Today, biotechnology and cloud computing and perhaps green energy are waves of the future. But what company or companies will be the giants in the industry? Your guess is as good as mine. Maybe better!

Especially when dealing with advanced technology it is very difficult to determine what path that technology will take. From time to time various companies will fall into and out of favor. Unless you are truly on the inside of the industry trying to invest in this arena can be damaging to your financial health.

Nevertheless it is important to understand what scientific and sociological changes will be affecting your generation and the next so that you can invest with an intelligent understanding of what that future may look like. You did not want to be invested heavily in buggy whip companies when the automobile was taking over from the horse and buggy! And the field of investing is littered with modern equivalents of buggy whip companies.

So what does the next few decades look like to me? Quite challenging. I foresee a boom in scientific knowledge with numerous practical applications. Computers are just starting to impact our lives. More and more appliances and homes will be run by computers and the cloud is only now coming into its own. Back in the 1940's there was a popular cartoon "Dick Tracy" in which Dick, the detective ,wore a radio/tv wrist watch.

In 2013 Samsung introduced just such a watch/video phone. Over the next 50 years our current science will probably look like the Model T automobile of the 1930's does to us today.

Likewise in biotechnology. In this industry we are probably way before the Model T era. To keep with the automobile analogy we are still in the tinkerer's garage. This industry was well on its way to becoming a stellar industry of the next century before the AIDS epidemic struck. With the research dollars being poured into the war on AIDS, cancer, heart disease, etc. the likely result in ten to twenty years will be a spectacular array of drugs and treatments from DNA revisions to artificial immune systems to growing replacement organs. As with any new technology just how the technological ball will bounce is unknowable. Attempts at prediction will probably be far off course. But we know enough already to know that there is a century plus of work to be done.

Space technology is also at the Model T state. The next century may see spectacular advances here as well although with cost cutting it is not clear that money will see its way to space exploration. Colonies on the moon and beyond are likely and the spin off of technology in other areas will continue to multiply. The computer of today would likely not exist but for WWII and the space race of the 1960's nor would many of our exotic alloys and other spin off products came from early space development. Much of our advanced plastics and ceramic technology would not have been developed but for the Apollo program. But there was a time in my career when I worked on translating space technology into commercial products and believe me when I tell you that was harder than you might think. One of our "great" achievements was to use the technology that put connectors on the end of cables of the Atlas rocket into Coleman camping tent pegs! Useful in a midnight rain storm not to have your tent peg come off the rope but not exactly rocket science--- well, I guess it was rocket science but not the kind of advances that ultimately came out of the program!

For those who think that the trajectory of science and technology is reaching its apex in my view the best is yet to come! The last century saw a dizzying growth of scientific and technical knowledge. Is it really only a hundred years since the advent of the automobile, airplane, computer, telephone, television and not much more for the electric light bulb! Considering the thousands of years man has existed on this planet the explosion of innovation from the 1700's to today (just a little over 300 years) is truly remarkable. And the next century seems to hold even greater promise.

As for demographic trends that will affect the economy we deal with the certain and the uncertain. First the certain. World population growth will not slow to zero in the next century. The pressure that this will put on our natural resources will be great. However, from the days of Malthus to the Club of Rome in the 1960's, those that have predicted disaster for the planet from population growth have simply been wrong. Not that anyone looking at the trend can help but be concerned. But the fact is that, so far, we have managed to stay ahead of the curve. I for one am not willing to bet money that we will not continue to so in the foreseeable future. Especially if other countries follow the lead of China and begin to promote zero population growth or perhaps even a decline in overall population.

In the United States we will be faced with more and more interrelationships with the world economies. It will likely be later in this century that we will see significant impact on our economy from this interrelationship. We have never been an island in the world economy. But more and more we have lost what insular status we did have. No longer can we adopt economic policies independent of the rest of the world.

Within our own country there are significant demographic factors that will result in a changing background for our economy. The Baby Boom generation is now starting to become senior citizens. Unless changes are made the potential for an inter-generational war is clearly present. The current Baby Boomers have a great deal of resentment for current seniors, who they feel they are supporting with their Social Security and Medicare taxes. If they feel that way now just wait until it is their turn! Want to bet they will change their tune? I do. The burden that the Baby Boomer turned senior will have on the younger generation will make their own burden at their ages seem like a feather!

My own guess? Seniors will find that their retirement ages are stretched from 65 to 70 or beyond. They will be forced to continue working in some capacity just to stay ahead of the game. The current bias against older workers will reverse and in the early decades of this century we will be hearing more and more about the value of experience. If my guess about the biotechnological revolution is correct and if this results in further expansion of life expectancy of the population then these pressures will be greater still. The percentage of population in the older ages will expand significantly. And not just in the US but in Japan, China and Europe as well.

Beyond this I am not prepared to go. It is exceedingly dangerous to project any trend more than a few years into the future. Time and again history has proved that the fears generated by those projecting into the future have been unfounded. Something, usually not predictable, except looking backward, tends to change events so that solutions are found.

In the 1970's there were many predicting the end of the industrial revolution from the rise in oil prices. Predictions for oil were in the hundreds of dollars a barrel. Something called the "Iron Law" was discussed. For economic growth to occur this Iron Law said that you needed a proportional increase in energy use. Pretty dismal stuff! Did not happen. Indeed energy rates in real dollars (even with most recent increases) are lower today than before the first energy crisis. Not that the crisis is over, just that those who plot economic events and then try to guess the future by drawing straight lines into the future are doomed to fail in those projections.

What you need to watch is the changing background. Try to spot where the changes are occurring and the effect on the economy. If the change is political then eventually that will find its way into economic effects. Try to filter out the noise of current events and watch the developing trends. Just as you use your knowledge of economic and business cycles as a background for investing, use the demographic and scientific developments to fill in part of the mosaic picture for you.

As for investing, my use of these factors is simply to avoid swimming against the stream. For example, brick and mortar book stores are having more and more trouble surviving in the 21st century. First, because of Amazon and other on line booksellers. Second, competition from Wal-Mart and Costco for best selling books and finally from Kindle, Nook and other book readers eliminating the hardback book altogether. Will this mean the end of the book as we know it? Probably not but it certainly will change the mix of how books are sold and in what form. To invest in a bookseller today is swimming against the tide of developments. For another example, I would not be favoring companies that need to derive growth from a teenage market in a period of expanding senior's market. Neither would I try to jump on the bandwagon of the senior market. Sam Walton is a good lesson giver here. While all the "major" retailers in the country were using their computers to project the "growth" area of the country, Sam Walton was working in the backwaters. Using my analogy of the teenage market vs. seniors, Sam let the big guys go after the seniors while he tackled the teenage market. They as they grew up he grew with them. Sometimes the biggest money is made doing what no one else wants to do. Sam Walton did not develop the small town, Middle America market because he had nostalgia for small town America, it was simply where he was and what he knew. Something often forgotten today is the fact that he was not alone in his attempt. People today forget Gibson Stores and Pamida that were doing what Sam Walton was doing. He just did it a lot better than they did! He had the touch, the knack of knowing his customers and his employees. The result has been one of the most remarkable success stories in the history of retailing.

Yet picking a Wal-Mart as an investment in the early days was a dangerous pick. When comparable companies were selling at low multiples to their earnings Wal-Mart has always sold at a big premium. And I can show you tens if not hundreds of companies that have had a similar "story" and have flopped. Two come to mind readily, Levitz was the warehouse furniture darling of the 1960's and Home Shopping Club another darling of the 1980's. Both skyrocketed and then fizzled as stock investments. Unfortunately for every IBM or Wal-Mart there are hundreds of flash and fizzle companies.

Finding an IBM or Wal-Mart is not successful investing, it is lucky investing. As the old saw goes, I would rather be lucky than good! But you cannot count on luck in your investing. If it happens to you then that is wonderful. As long as it is good luck that is! Yet it is the story of IBM, Wal-Mart or Marion Labs or Apple or Microsoft or Dell or any one of a hundred others that the brokers use to sell the public the thousands of also rans that dot the investment market place.

Use knowledge of demographics and scientific development with care in your investments. Don't try to outsmart the market trying to spot the next IBM or Wal-Mart. That is truly a sucker's game and not for investors.

5.2 WAR AND PEACE

Ask most people today and they would say there have been two major wars in the last century – WWI and II, plus Korea, Vietnam, Gulf I and II, Afghanistan and perhaps some would throw in Bosnia, Nicaragua, Panama, Angola and a few others.

My view is a little different. I think we have had one major hundred year plus war. Starting in the early 1800's when the large powers began gobbling up smaller nations into colonial empires and morphing at the end of the last century with the disintegration of those same colonial empires. Speaking in economic terms it is interesting that these empires were created beginning in the 1790's with the industrial revolution and that they are crumbling as the larger nations in the world are moving into a post industrial society.

I will not pretend to be an historian or an expert on the inter-relationships that may be at work here. But starting with WWI let's go through what has happened. WWI resulted in tens of millions of military deaths. It was the first total world war where whole populations were involved. War was no longer left to the soldiers and sailors. The greatest impact was the destabilization both politically and economically that resulted. There is no doubt that the rise of Hitler and Stalin can both be traced directly to WWI. The Czar lost control of his people who became fed up with WWI and that in turn created the revolution that has affected the world since 1917. Likewise the terms of surrender of Germany after WWI resulted in one of the worst inflationary spirals and economic depressions in Germany that the world has seen. Out of that economic despair the German people reached out for anyone who might have an answer. Regrettably for the world, Hitler answered their call.

As for the great depression it may well have had its seeds in the destabilization wrought by WWI. All of which in turn laid the ground work for the even more horrific war, WWII.

I wrote the above before reading George Will's commencement address to the 1991 graduating class at Duke University, reprinted as the lead article in the Fall 1991 issue of "American Scholar" magazine. Will makes a similar point. That the troubles in the Balkans that preceded WWI was the starting point for much of the history of the rest of the century.

And World War II in turn set in motion even more destabilization. Fortunately we learned a thing or two from WWI and instead of oppressing the losers in WWII we built them up with the Marshall Plan and restored their dignity and place in the world.

Much the same is likely to happen through the next few decades in eastern Europe and the former Russian Soviet Union. The former chairman of Volkswagen commented that the OECD which administered the Marshall Plan still exists and should be used for a new Marshall Plan for Eastern Europe. That, however, has not come to pass. And the recovery of Eastern Europe has therefore been slower than Germany and Italy and Japan after WWII.

With the cold war ending the world has another chance for genuine peace. Many of the small wars that have plagued us since WWII were nothing but sponsored gang warfare. The super powers, knowing that their nuclear arsenals prevented them from head on confrontation, chose instead to fight each other through proxy nations and to some extent that continues today. And the terrorism of today had its roots in this proxy warfare with Al Qaeda having been born out of the CIA sponsored resistance to the Russians in Afghanistan. Heads of small nations know they can play one side against the other and today that is the US vs. Europe vs. Russia vs. China. They learned quickly how to do this to their advantage. Just like siblings who know what buttons to push with one another or their parents to get their way, these third world leaders know just what buttons to push that would open the coffers of the super powers pouring in money, arms or whatever their hearts desired.

Will genuine peace come to pass? I certainly hope so although history is not kind in this regard. If we can strengthen the economic ties that bind one nation to another then there is real hope. To establish true peace we must give nations more to lose than to gain by engaging in war. That won't be easy but it may be possible. It is far too early in the process to predict which way the world will turn and recent rise in religious terrorism extends the difficulties as does the spread of nuclear weapons from North Korea to Pakistan and India and soon Iran.

As the world adjusts there will be ups and downs economically, some of which may be severe. We can only hope that the promise of peaceful profit will prevail over the profit of war.

Perhaps as never before in the history of the world we stand in prospect of genuine peace. It is hard to imagine what rewards could be forthcoming for the peoples of the world if that peace is truly achieved. Investors will be among those most generously rewarded if we enter this new peaceful era.

For an investor it is a time of great opportunity and danger. The investor must be careful to watch and gauge the progress of the peace development, becoming neither too euphoric nor too pessimistic. It is a time when realists will make the profits and avoid the losses.

One aspect of the new era of peace will be the continued breakdown of the nation state. I suspect that once the history of the last 250 years is written it will emphasize two major changes. The first was the change from agricultural economics to industrial economies and the second is the change from industrial to post industrial (service and technology based) economies. I use the term post industrial because it is still not clear into what this will evolve. We talk today of the service economy and the technology/ information age, but the true dimensions of this change I do not believe will be known for some time to come.

A few years ago I became interested in collecting antiquities from the BCE. era, principally small fragments of pottery from archaeological sites around the Mediterranean. In the course of pursuing this interest I returned to studies that I had not touched since college. The more I read the more I was impressed by just how little the world changed from 10,000 BCE. to 1500AD. There were developments certainly, but the human that lived in 10,000 BCE would not have had nearly the difficulty living in 1500 AD that the human living in 1500AD would have were they to be brought back to life today.

The rise of the industrial economy in the West created the boom in colonial development. Both for raw materials and markets for finished goods. Development of trading block and spheres of influence all had commercial impact.

As the world moved beyond the industrial era the need for colonial empires diminished. And the great wars of the last century finished off the colonial empires once and for all. Indeed since WWII I can think of no instance of nations joining together to form a larger nation (the amalgamation of Germany and of Europe under the Euro are exceptions). It is much easier to cite examples of large nations breaking apart, from the Soviet Union to Yugoslavia. In Canada there is the drive for independence for Quebec and I doubt that over the next 100 years the United States will find itself immune from these pressures, in part because of the influx of Mexican and Asian immigrants that are already changing the mix of peoples of the United States.

As the threat of global war diminishes and nations focus on their individual economic interests we can expect great changes in relationships between nations, with new trading patterns and markets developing. This too, the global investor must watch with care. As the decades roll by the investor will need a much wider global focus than ever before. Both to participate in the opportunities and to protect against pitfalls.

CHAPTER SIX. SOME UNCOMMON THOUGHTS

INTRODUCTION:

We have covered a lot of ground up to this point, much of it general in its nature. Hopefully you will have seen its purpose, to paint the background against which we will draw in the specifics of our investment plans. In this chapter you will find some analysis that becomes more specific. Over my 50 odd years of investing I have tried and rejected a number of techniques for investing. And I have developed some thinking that differs from much that you will read from others who would seek to pass on investment wisdom. I leave to you whether you find these uncommon thoughts of use in your investing.

As you pursue your investment program I am sure you will develop some uncommon thoughts of your own. The ability to spot a small, but profitable, niche in the investment world can result in the best investment results. For example, every so often the computer jocks will push the panic button and there will be a flash crash. If you are quick you may be able to pick up some stock you are interested in at 20% or more discounts to just a few minutes before. This is not for the faint of heart but if you happen to be at your computer when one of these events occurs you may profit handsomely. Same is true when market panics occur no matter if for good reasons or not. If you do not join in the panic but follow through with your plan you may get a position far cheaper than usual. I find that down markets end up making me the most money. Because I can sell (at least in nontaxable accounts) positions that hold up and replace them with positions that have been hit hard but which have full recovery potential over time. Likewise in a taxable account if the market decline is severe I may be able to lock in a tax loss (being careful of the 31 day before and after Wash Sale rule).

It is said of Lord Keynes, liberal economic guru for the last 75 years, that he spent his early morning hours engaged in an international currency/commodity trading system by which he made and preserved a fortune. The rest of the day he spent on other matters. Exactly what his system was and how he implemented it I have no idea or even if I did it might not work today. What I have learned is that those who will spend time and energy spotting opportunities that others know little about have a better than average change of better than average investment returns.

6.1 ALLOCATIONS: CASH,BONDS AND STOCKS

Talk to a stockbroker, read an investment publication or watch a financial program and you will inevitably hear recommendations about how much you should allocate to cash, bonds and stocks. Beyond that others will allocate some to gold, some to international bonds, international equities, commodities etc.

I believe that most allocation systems will not help your investment performance. I do believe in diversifying your investments – not putting all your eggs in one basket.

But as I will explain in a moment I believe that the allocation systems are an attempt to duck making a decision as to where an investor should be at a particular time.

My own investment plan calls for me to be in stocks or cash (including bonds) with one exception. In a period of high inflation special rules apply. This is the only time that I would consider real estate, gold or debt (as a debtor not a creditor) as an investment option. Also, because I can never be absolutely certain what may happen I believe in keeping a minimum of 25% cash position at all times and usually a 75% (but never less than a 25%) stock position at all times. That is not including emergency cash position which everyone should establish and keep in FDIC safe accounts. There is no magic in these ratios. You could decide on an 80%/20% ratio especially if you have a large portfolio and long time horizon. But you will see shortly why fixing a ratio and staying with it can be important to investment success.

Also, I do not vary my investment plans significantly based on my age or situation. What I do vary is the protective cash position that I keep for emergencies or short term needs e.g., purchase of car, vacation etc. I call this my cash reservoir since it serves as the financial equivalent of a water reservoir; that is it fills up in good times and is available to take down in bad times.

Contrast my approach to that of most investment houses. Most brokers and authors on this subject start by analyzing your family position, age and economic situation. A reasonable start. I would do the same. The difference is that they then proceed to allocate the types of investments you should have depending on whether you are young and single or married with college age kids or a retired couple. Their allocation is predictable. For the young they go for aggressive growth. For the retirement couple they go for traditionally conservative income type investments. The mix they recommend can vary greatly but the approach is invariably the same.

In contrast, I believe that everyone needs a financial reservoir. Just how big this reservoir needs to be will depend on the factors most advisors consider. For the single person and the young couple the first need is emergency cash. Sometimes this is guesstimated at six months of salary or one months of salary for every $10,000 in annual income --so for someone making $120,000 they would need a full year of emergency cash. My view is you have to look at your own needs and situation. If you are in a job that is easy to move to another then you may need less emergency cash than someone who could be out of work a couple of years in a bad economy. And if you have a house mortgage that needs consideration in an emergency budget.

Personally I tried to keep at least two to three years of reservoir cash while I was putting my children through college and graduate school. Since I live primarily off investment income I have to be prepared for three to four years or more of a bad market. For the period from 2000 to 2020 this entire period could be one of great difficulty for investments. I do not want to liquidate my investments in a down market for living expenses. Therefore I keep more cash. Of course I do not keep this cash in a sock under my mattress. Depending on the state of interest rates I keep it in insured money market funds or in short term governments, high grade municipals and a portion may be in longer term governments or in high yield securities. Since 2008 and extending now to 2013 the Federal Reserve has been taking money from savers to give to the profligate. Robin Hood, but in reverse. It may make economic sense but it is sure difficult for savers. In this period I am using a dumbbell approach. I keep 75% of cash in low (or no) yielding FDIC protected accounts and 25% in high risk but high yield assets so that the blended return is somewhere north of 5% for this entire balance at a time when money markets are yielding practically zero. I try to keep most of this in tax free accounts limiting my taxable income and using tax free municipal bonds where possible. A portion may even be in high yielding common stocks where dividends from utilities or other common stocks with good dividend yield gives a more attractive return.

How I apportion my cash reservoir depends on economic conditions, interest rates present and anticipated. But I keep clearly in mind that this is my "cash" fund and not my "investment" fund. The purpose of the cash fund is to permit me to meet expected and unexpected expenses over an extended period of time without having to dip into my investment fund. When the stock market drops 50% (and it has and will again) this lets me sleep comfortably at night. Maybe not as comfortably as I did at higher levels, but comfortably enough.

As for the investment fund I handle this aggressively and plan to do so at every stage of my life. I will move from one type of investment to another strictly to achieve maximum return on my investments, with my 25% a year compounded return objective clearly in mind. I know it is unlikely I will make that 25% but by reaching for it I have achieved far better returns than if I had selected an easier target.

It is not the purpose of this chapter to discuss how I handle my investment fund. That will come just a little later. The important thing to understand is that I have only two funds and I recommend that you do the same. The first fund is the cash reservoir fund. It is protective. My personal reservoir has changed greatly over the years. When I was making a large and steady salary with a three year contract to protect me, I kept a smaller reservoir than when I went into private practice. There I had not only my own daily living needs and protection against unexpected expense but I had to protect my law practice income as well. This fluctuated and needed its own cash reservoir to protect my investment fund. After leaving private law practice to handle my own investments I needed more of a reservoir than when I was in corporate law practice but less than when I was in private law practice. With children in college the reservoir grew even larger and once they were on their own the reservoir decreased again. The cash reservoir needed is a constantly moving target and always only an estimate so when estimating do so on the high side!

Types of cash holdings can be tailored to your needs as well. When I was younger I inherited E Bonds purchased during WWII. For many years I kept these and rolled them forward. Contrary, I might add, to the investment wisdom at the time. I could have cashed them in but had I done so at the time I would have owed nearly 70%

tax on the accumulated interest. Since these had been held since WWII that meant a big tax hit. Instead I kept them in my cash reservoir, knowing if I ever fell on hard times that I could cash them in then at a much lower tax rate. While I never fell on hard times economically, at least not yet, I did take these E Bonds down when I was moving from private practice into my investment career. There was a period of a year when my tax rates were relatively low and because of market conditions I was not taking down large capital gains. As a result I managed to cash these in at an average tax rate of 15%.

I would probably have kept these to this day but for the fact that after forty years I had to cash them in for H bonds and start taking current income. Had I been able to continue to accumulate the income tax free I would still be holding them.

During college years for my children we bought EE Bonds which could be used tax free to pay for tuition. After using this for this purpose there was still some left and those continue to sit in my cash fund until they no longer will earn interest, sometime in 2022.

Another useful investment I included in the cash reservoir was a single premium life insurance policy on our children. I took these out when the children were young for two purposes. First to give them guaranteed insurability to the principal amount. Second because at the time they had wonderful tax advantages including the ability to borrow the principal amount tax free (a feature since stopped for new issues). Finally I plan to give these policies to my children when the time is right and they will then have a protected insurance base and a nice investment nest egg for their own cash reservoirs.

I tell these stories for a simple purpose. That is to encourage you to separate your cash reservoir from your investment funds and to look carefully at your cash position on a regular basis to be sure it is fulfilling its protective purpose. Every dollar you keep in your cash reservoir will earn you far less than in your investment fund. So you want to keep it only at the level it needs to be to protect your emergency needs. Put in various investments that may accumulate tax free (like EE Bonds or a Roth IRA) those funds will then be available in troubled times at a time of lower tax rates. Of course your needs may not come at a time of lower taxes so you need to keep some available funds for emergencies that do not result from job loss such as illness, car accidents, college education costs, etc. Only you can determine what level reservoir you will need. Hopefully these examples will give you a start in thinking about how much you should set aside for these purposes.

Once you have set aside your cash reservoir you are left with the funds you can invest. The traditional wisdom will tell you to allocate, some to cash, some to bonds and some to stocks. Within bonds and stocks some will allocate further between so-called conservative and so-called aggressive investments. I do not agree.

I believe that with some important exceptions (to be discussed later) that you should allocate only between cash (or short term bonds) and stock investments. Why? Because the standard rules for making allocations were created in the 1920's through the

1950's. They worked then. We were an agricultural / industrial society. We had very distinct business cycles. A successful investor could anticipate moves in the cycle, moving to bonds at the top of the cycle and back to stocks when the cycle bottomed. And this worked beautifully if you were right in your cycle analysis.

Today, conditions are very different. We are now a service / postindustrial society with a different set of cyclical conditions. The markets are faster moving due to a variety of reasons. Among these are the power of computers, global investors, hedge funds and a host of instruments such as derivatives that can move markets quickly. Sometimes too quickly as the advent of the flash crash has shown. The result is that bonds do not lead stocks by nearly as much as they used to. There are times, even years, when it would be better to be in bonds than stocks. For the most part you are far better off in stocks than in bonds, or you should be in cash instead. So for the time being at least I reject the traditional wisdom of putting so much in cash, bonds and stocks. Only if you are a nontaxable pension fund, trust or other fund with fiduciary obligations should you use the allocation formula. Even then I have my doubts but your lawyers will probably sleep better if you follow the traditional rules and allocate.

Within the stock portfolio should you allocate between classes of stock? Again I don't think so. You need to be adequately diversified. This I believe in firmly. As I will explain later a good mutual fund can do this for you admirably and with the advent of ETF's this is another vehicle to diversify. Beyond diversification in a number of companies I think you need to focus on market developments and be in the correct types of securities for the market conditions. For example, if the dollar is falling and foreign stock markets are robust when ours are weak then you should be at least to some extent weighted more to global securities and in your U.S. investments you should be focused on the larger capitalization stocks with a big foreign exposure. Often you do not need to buy international stocks but U.S. stocks with big international exposure. This international exposure can be obtained through ETF of mutual funds as well as individual companies. There are times when closed end mutual funds offer excellent buys, other times when small capitalization stocks are the place to be. Other times when they are the place to avoid. All of this will be covered in detail later.

Allocation based on these considerations is what you should be doing. If there are values in stocks then limit the cash position in your portfolio (keeping in mind that you should maintain 25% in cash at all times). You may vary the amount in stocks and cash based on your view of the state of the market or to start working your way in or out as conditions change. But your returns will suffer greatly if you try to play it too safe. Or if you think you know the trend of the market and find later you were wrong. In the end your desire for safety may see your capital erode, exactly what you are trying to avoid.

Don't misunderstand my position. I am not advocating you take foolish risks or gambles, but knowing the probabilities in the market I suggest you take carefully considered calculated risks to maximize your return and protect your investment funds from the ravages of inflation and taxes.

The purpose of this chapter is not to discuss how you do all of the above. The only purpose of this chapter is to warn you off the traditional allocation formulas. You will hear and read a lot about these. And of course brokers love them! After all every time that you adjust your portfolio to a new allocation they earn a fee. I do not question their honesty in believing in allocation strategies, I merely point out that it does not hurt their business. As you can see from the discussion above I do advocate allocating but on a different basis. I allocate first to the reservoir the amount of cash that is needed for protection. Within that fund allocations are made to some investments that can be cashed in in bad economic times at low tax rates (e.g. E Bonds) and investments that can be cashed in overnight in the event of an emergency. The second allocation is to the investment fund. Within that fund that allocation is based on my sense of the market and where the opportunities may lie. If it looks like foreign stocks have the edge then a reasonable amount may be allocated there. If closed end funds are at a big discount then money may be allocated to them. If small cap stocks look like the place to be then an appropriate amount is allocated there. Since no investor can accurately predict the future I will never go whole hog in one area or another. But my allocation is always based on maximizing returns and achieving my objective for my investment fund of a 25% annual return over time.

6.2 AFTER TAX REFORM

Before the Tax Reform Act of 1986 I was a very different investor. I used some mutual funds but for the most part I invested in individual stocks. What changed? The tax laws changed. And every twist and turn of the tax law since then have caused me to adjust my investment thinking.

Before 1986 there was a significant advantage to capital gains for the smaller investor. The Democrats would like us to believe that capital gains are only for the rich and they are once again trying to eliminate any preference in tax policy for capital gains. To a point they are right but in one very key respect they are wrong. When the law changed in 1986 the increase for a big investor went from 25% to 28 or 31%. Not a big deal. Especially since most of these people had large incomes outside of their investments, now taxed a far lower rate.

The smaller investor suffered a significant change. In many cases the capital gains tax was increased from 35% to 100% over what it had been before. When state taxes were considered in most states the result was even worse. For example, take an investor previously taxed at a top rate of 33%. In one year they realized a big capital gain (for them) of $50,000 that is added on to the top of their usual income. For simplicity say that the entire $50,000 was taxed at a rate of 33% (Federal and State). Before 1986 60% of the gain would have been excluded leaving only $20,000 to be taxed with a tax of less than $7,000. Under the new tax rates the tax would be more than $13.000. An increase in tax of nearly 100%. The Bush tax changes helped the situation but the Democrats are bound and determined to let those changes expire.

What does that have to do with investing in individual stocks in a taxable account? A lot! First of all the change gave added emphasis to using retirement fund vehicles such as an IRA, 401(k) or other tax advantaged plans. Next, since capital gains will eat more heavily into your capital base you will need a more aggressive strategy to give you the same amount of after tax, after inflation income. And this return is not likely to come from owning ATT, GE or Coca Cola. I wish it were that easy. Instead the government has forced you into a more risky and aggressive strategy. In which case the diversification of mutual funds and ETF's becomes more important. Finally, the amount of trading that you are now forced to do to try and protect your capital will result in not only increased taxes but increased trading costs as well. For the average, or even above average, investor this can be significant. The transaction costs can eat up a significant part of your return if you are not careful. Transaction costs in no load mutual funds are minimal by comparison and therefore they have the advantage.

So the 1986 Tax Act (and ones that have followed or are proposed) has forced the intelligent investor to become an aggressive trader (not day trader by the way!) of stocks, taking larger risks for larger returns to make the same after tax, after inflation, return. I don't like it but having no choice have to deal with it.

Maybe someday Congress will wake up and adopt a sensible capital gains policy for middle class Americans once again. I doubt it. Current policy seems directed at the slow eradication of the middle class polarizing America into the super-rich and the poor. Not a good omen if history is any judge. Usually when this happens heads roll. Why they want to accomplish this is beyond me and beyond this section as well. Except to point out that more and more taxes, hidden and not so hidden, are being heaped on the middle class. The primary reason is the same as it was for Willy Sutton, the bank robber. Asked why he robbed banks Sutton replied "because that is where the money is." All you and I can do is to try to anticipate and adjust to these changing winds as best we can. For those with money to invest this means you have two choices. Follow traditionally conservative policies and see your capital eroded by taxes and inflation in which case I recommend that you forget investing, spend your capital and enjoy it. Better you than Washington D.C. Or you can become more aggressive in your investing with a shot at protecting your capital and making a decent after tax/after inflation return. The choice is yours. It is not a great choice but it is real life today.

For the immediate future it is my conclusion that using a discount broker to lower transaction costs, no load and closed end mutual funds or ETF's is the best way to proceed. In my case I do all of these. I still own some individual stocks, mostly speculative in nature, but prefer to diversify with closed end, no load mutual funds and ETF's. One warning on mutual funds. Because they distribute capital gains as well as income owning them in a taxable account can make it very difficult to do year-end tax planning since most distribute capital gains right at calendar year end. For that reason I prefer to hold these in my nontaxable accounts where possible.

6.3 IRA's, 401(k) AND OTHER TAX FREE ACCOUNTS

Reading the advertisements for IRAs (Individual Retirement Accounts) is interesting. Almost all of them utilize tables or graphs showing the accumulated account value over time. Most use this as an encouragement to invest in these accounts early in life. The point is valid. By using compounding the values projected are usually quite large. The problem with most of these projections is that they do not take into account inflation. And almost none take taxes into account. Even in tax deferred accounts taxes occur at the end (when, except for Roth IRAs) you must start making annual taxable withdrawals (RMD – Required Mandatory Distributions). The result for most of these is far less spectacular when the real world effects are plugged into the tables and charts.

My own analysis is that putting as much into IRA (particularly Roth IRAs which have no mandatory withdrawal and accumulate tax free with no tax at the end and with estate tax advantages too—at least as of now) or similar tax sheltered vehicles as you can and as early as you can is very worthwhile. Especially in the current tax environment which is unfriendly and likely to get more so for investors. The tax on your capital makes investing outside a tax shelter extremely difficult and for most people nearly impossible to achieve a good after tax, after inflation return.

Within the IRA or other tax free account I believe you should invest in aggressive growth funds using very little market timing. Rebalancing your portfolio in early May and early October is a good idea. Remember that, except in a Roth IRA, Uncle Sam is sharing the risk with you since you did not pay tax on the money you are investing. So, if you have a loss Uncle Sam shares in that loss eventually. If you have a gain Uncle Sam will share in that as well but not for a long time.

We will discuss this subject at greater length later. For now do your own analysis with whatever investment, inflation and tax rates you choose. I think you will conclude, as I have, that you should use the most aggressive strategy in your tax sheltered investments. Provided of course you have created your cash reservoir so you will not have to dip into investment funds until you are ready to do so. After all these are your long term investment funds. You should not be planning to need these for a long time to come. By the time you do need them, with a reasonable amount of skill and luck you will have built a very large portfolio for yourself, only a small part of which you will want to take down to live and enjoy with the rest continuing to grow for you.

Two quick words more on the subject. First, the government allows or is thinking about allowing you to withdraw funds for things like a house, college or medical bills. While this is nice it is also a trap. Uncle Sam knows just how valuable those plans can be and they want you to take them down earlier rather than later. From your standpoint the IRA (probably a Roth) should be your first long term investment, up to the maximum allowed. If you can use another tax sheltered account such as a 401(k) and especially if your contributions are matched by your employer then this may be your first or second long term investment. Furthermore don't plan to withdraw funds for any purpose. Even when you turn 59 ½ and can make withdrawals without penalty, you should plan to take out only the absolute minimum required each year after you reach age 70 . These are current rules and could change by the way. If you have followed an aggressive strategy and had even reasonable luck then the capital base you will be withdrawing from will produce an enormous return for you over the rest of your lifetime. In a later section on this subject you will see some examples of this strategy that will make clear that you want to build these accounts as rapidly as you can, invest them aggressively and plan to make no withdrawals until you retire and then only that amount you really need or are obligated to withdraw. At 70 ½ under current rules you will be required to start a withdrawal process (except for Roth IRAs) but this can extend over the remainder of your life.

There is a lot of advertising today about the need to take out insurance against the day you might have to enter a nursing home. I think most of this is bunk. There is really no way to know what you will need out in time. Conditions will change, of that you can be sure. A well thought out IRA plan with an aggressive investment program will probably produce for you far more than you will ever need in your retirement with a very large balance to pass on to your family, charities or whomsoever you wish. Merely setting up the account will not do it, you need to go for the gold by investing aggressively as well. And be prepared for major and sometimes painful dips in the market along the way.

I suppose before going much further I should say a word or two about aggressive investing. That sounds dangerous. It can be unless you plan wisely. But even a badly handled aggressive plan is probably better than a so-called conservative approach. Remember Enron, GM, Lehman Brothers? When names like those are not safe who knows what may befall GE or P&G or Johnson and Johnson? As you know by now, I believe that any investment program extending more than a couple of years will produce unacceptable results unless it produces a minimum of 22% a year in return. And there is no way to achieve a 22% return without being aggressive.

Now there is a difference between being aggressive and gambling. Sometimes in investing the line is thin but it is there. For example, knowing that over time (15 to 25 years) aggressive no load growth mutual funds have historically produced at 25% a year gain on a buy and hold basis, gives you a solid framework to shoot for such gains. If you can do a little market timing as well you may be able to increase those returns to 35% a year. No, not every year or even every ten years but over a lifetime of investing. Add to that a mix of closed end funds and some arbitrage strategies and you can approach a possible 50% a year return. You probably will not do that well over a 25-50 year investment career…but some have and you might too. To achieve these returns you will have some lousy years and some spectacular years. But if you know what you are doing and why you are doing it and keep control of your emotions so as not to panic and be out of the market when you should be in (or vice versa) then you can make an aggressive plan work for you. That is the way to make an IRA, 401(k) or other tax deferred plan work miracles for you.

6.4 MORE ON TAXES

As we have gone along I have from time to time made a point or two about taxes. Once you have set aside the maximum you can in non-taxable or tax deferred investments you will have to contend with taxes on the rest of your investment program. And once you reach 70 ½ you will have to deal with taxes from all but the Roth IRAs in your IRA and 401(k) accounts. As we have seen the impact of taxes can make achieving a good return very difficult indeed.

You need to study about taxes so that you will know the rules and how you can use them to your advantage. And these rules are constantly changing, sometimes in ways that require you to totally rethink what you are doing.

An example of tax rules you need to consider is the rule on using your losses to offset realized gains plus $3,000 of ordinary income. While this can carry over into another year it is a limited but useful benefit to taking a tax loss. In a down year you need to take advantage of this by realizing enough losses to offset any gains and perhaps some ordinary income, particularly if you are in the upper tax brackets. You do not need to get out of the market to do this. Let's say you have a $20,000 loss in one mutual fund and a $10,000 gain in another. You can move these into a similar mutual fund, offset the gain and loss and have $10,000 in net losses of which $3000 can offset this year's ordinary income and leave you $7,000 to apply the following year. Of course eventually you have to pay the taxes but not until later. The only time you would not want to do this would be when you think that taxes in the future will be greater than they are at present but even then a bird in the hand may be better than one in the bush.

With mutual funds you need to know the various rules that apply to distributions and how they are taxed. Currently there are several possible techniques. Specific identification of shares sold is almost always the best from your standpoint. Needless to say Uncle Sam does not advertise this and pushes its average cost rule. And Congress may force the issue.

In your taxable investments you need to keep adjusting your mutual fund costs by amounts that are distributed, taxed and reinvested. I hate to think how many people fail to do this and end up paying far more in tax than they need to. New rules that require brokers to keep track of the cost basis of stocks and mutual funds held in street name should help in the future.

There is also a rule about so-called "wash sales" which has been mentioned elsewhere. This rule says that if you buy and sell the same security within a thirty day period either side of the tax loss sale then you cannot take any loss that results. If you have a gain you can sell a stock and rebuy it one minute later and you must report the gain. If you do the same for a loss it is a wash sale and no loss for tax purposes results. If, however, you sell one stock and buy a similar stock and then go back and reverse it 32 days later then you can take the loss. This works especially well with bonds where you can sell a treasury security of one month and buy one of the next month and take, for tax purposes, the loss. The securities are from an investment standpoint virtually identical. The difference is that you still have a fully invested position but with a tax loss. With mutual funds you can sell shares in one fund and immediately buy a very similar fund and then 32 days later go back to the original fund. Of course you want to be in no load mutual funds to do this and avoid transaction costs.

This book is not intended to teach a tax course. You need to read about the subject and become as well versed as possible on tax laws that apply to your investing. There are annual books that are quite good and the Kiplinger Tax Letter is very helpful as well. If you do learn about taxes you will find that there is a lot you can do to lessen the tax bite or at least to postpone it. If you do not study the rules I can assure you that you will pay dearly for not applying yourself. Since Uncle Sam knows that most of us hate taxes and hate even more studying about them the rules are generally set up so that the lazy taxpayer loses.

If you do not know the rules and apply them to your advantage the "default" rule will assuredly be in the favor the IRS and not in your favor. For example, I have mentioned mutual funds. If you own 1000 shares of a mutual fund at an average price of $20 a share and half your shares were bought at $10 a share and half at $30 a share and the current price is $25 if you want to withdraw $5000 to do so you plan to sell 200 shares. Using the government "default" rule you will realize a $5 profit on each share. If, however, you know the rules and you elect to use an alternative method (assuming that is still permitted at the time you read this) then you can withdraw the same $5000 and have a $5 loss per share instead! You simply elect to use the specific identification rule. Then you identify the shares sold as the ones you paid $30 for and the result is a $5 per share loss. The choice is yours. And if you really need $5000 after taxes for some reason you will need to sell more than 200 shares to net, after taxes, your $5000 or if you take the smart approach you can sell fewer than 200 shares and end up after taxes with the $5000 you need.

If your follow the lazy "default" route the rule that applies will always cost you more than you needed to pay. Trust Uncle Sam and he will take you to the cleaners every time. Keep in mind I am not talking about cheating. I think it is incredibly stupid to cheat on your taxes. What I am talking about is applying the rules that you are allowed, sometimes even encouraged, to apply to your tax affairs.

Learn about the tax rules that affect your investing. J.K. Lasser publishes a Tax Guide annually and it is a very good source to learn about taxes as it applies to your investing and your life in general. I use tax software to do my taxes but every year I pick up a copy of this guide as I find it invaluable during the tax year plus a quick guide to what is new and changing.

Lasser is a reader friendly way to learn. But you have to steel yourself to the task and you will be amply rewarded for the effort. Once you learn the rules you have to stay on top of changes but that is not nearly so difficult as learning the rules in the first place. Kiplinger Tax Letter is another good source of update but it may be that Lasser is really all you will need. Failing to watch the tax effect of what you are doing will eat into your real investment returns. So pay attention….or pay up! The choice is yours.

6.5 LOOK FOR STRATEGIES

There are many efficiencies in the market. As we discussed earlier some believe that the market is so efficient that the only way to intelligently make money is through so called index funds or a dart board approach. Throwing a dart at a listing of stocks and compiling a portfolio from 20 or so darts. Not recommended by the way!

Recognizing that efficiencies make beating the overall market challenging there are inefficient pockets that can be exploited to your advantage.

In a later chapter we will discuss in detail one of these pockets, the closed end mutual fund. There are other areas as well that you may come across. For me there are sufficient opportunities in closed end funds to focus on this approach.

You will recall that there are open end mutual funds and closed end mutual funds. In an open end fund the manager sells stock to new investors at the net asset value of the fund, usually the close of the market the day the money is deposited for investment. Likewise when money is withdrawn it comes out at the net asset value at the end of the market day. The number of shares of stock of open end mutual funds go up and down depending on whether investors as a whole are putting new money into the fund or taking it out.

In a closed end fund shares of stock are sold just like any new issue of a company. The money received, less the costs of raising the money, becomes the net asset value of the fund. Thereafter the price of the stock depends not on the net asset value of the fund's investments but on what investors are willing to pay for that stock. Usually the amount they are willing to pay is less than the net asset value. There are many reasons for this which will be discussed later. Sometimes they will pay a premium for the stock, usually a dumb move. Indeed buying a closed end fund new issue is usually a really dumb move. Both aspects will be covered later but for now just note that you almost never want to buy a closed end fund for a premium or as part of a new issue.

In 1989 the SEC released a long awaited report on closed end performance. In this report it found that buying closed end funds at their initial offering prices is one of the fastest and surest ways of losing money on Wall Street. The reason is that closed end funds initial public offerings are priced to include hefty sales commissions, usually 7 to 8%. The day after the offering the net asset value will drop by not only the commission but also the cost of the offering. Also the attention paid to the new issue may keep its value up for a short while but within 6 months generally these new issues will carry a hefty discount to net asset value and that is the time to consider one you otherwise consider worthwhile.

Because the manager of an open end fund never knows when the money will be withdrawn in excess of money coming in some of the money in the fund that would otherwise be invested has to be kept in short term cash to meet possible net redemptions.

This means that instead of 100% of your money working for you 5% or more is usually left sitting in a checking account equivalent against the possibility of withdrawals exceeding new investments. In a time when the market is plunging the manager may be forced to increase this amount since redemptions in such periods are almost certain to increase. So managers of these funds contribute to the downward pressure on stocks much in the same way margin calls add to downward pressure.

The manager of the closed end fund does not have to keep an eye on this problem. He does, however, have a problem the open end manager does not have. If the discount of market value to net asset value becomes too wide the closed end fund manager may face a shareholder revolt that can result in open ending the fund. Several funds have in the past had this raid conducted on them and most have tried to implement mechanisms to shrink the discount, typically a guaranteed pay out of 10% a year. They can also repurchase shares pocketing the high discount for their shareholders. Of course this shrinks the fund so when market conditions permit they will often offer more shares which may or may not be dilutive to existing shareholders. These protective measures work to the advantage of the managers but not necessarily the smart investor. The smart investor wants to see the discount widen and shrink. It is this process, about which more in detail shortly, that makes for the inefficiency that permits the smart investor the opportunity to make above average returns.

One study of closed end funds by a finance professor at University of Alabama showed the returns from certain strategies using closed end funds from 1965 to 1985, this was not a good period for the stock market by the way. In real terms the stock market measured by its large cap indexes declined substantially during this period. The result when compared to a buy and hold strategy or use of an index fund was significant. Significant enough to require any serious investor to think about adopting a form of closed end fund strategy.

As you will see when we get to the specifics of my investment program I utilize closed end funds together with market timing to maximize my returns. There are times I do not make a move in the market for several years and other times I may move much more frequently. Market conditions dictate the best strategy. This calls for discipline and a solid plan but the rewards are truly worth it.

Over time it may be that the closed end fund will disappear or the advantages of the closed end fund strategy will diminish and for a 401(k) this strategy is not available. Only open end funds are offered there. In a self directed IRA, Roth or Traditional, the closed end strategy will be available is you use a discount broker and maintain an IRA where you can buy and sell stocks and bonds for your IRA.

The one thing certain in investing is that change will occur. My grandfather, who got me interested in investing, would be truly puzzled by what I do today, until we could talk about it. If we did then he would understand quickly. What worked for him in the 1930's to 1950's does not always work today. And what worked for me in the 1980's and 1990's does not work as well in the 21st Century. The fundamental rules will still apply but the details of the game will vary. Old stocks and old investment products will fade away and new stocks and new products will come along.

The wise investor will reject the old when the time comes and will cautiously adopt the new when it makes sense. Making changes is the hardest thing to do in investing. Just when you get comfortable with an approach something, like taxes or inflation or war or scientific change, occurs that throws your current plan in a cocked hat. Yet if you allow your investment plan to blow with every new wind that comes along that will prove disastrous as well. So always keep testing old strategies, looking for new ones and never letting greed or fear drive your investment plans. Make moves slowly but decisively once you are sure of your approach.

After a few years investing you will know what I am talking about. Until you have a few years under your belt you will have no earthly idea what I am saying. This is one aspect of investing that one generation cannot pass on to the next. We all had to learn it; usually the hard way! Hopefully you will not have to do that.

6.6 BROKERS – PAY FOR WHAT YOU NEED

When I started investing, in the 1950's, you dealt with a broker who charged a fixed schedule fee for stock transactions. Brokers competed on the basis of service, not price.

In the 1960's all that changed. Now brokers are able to negotiate and discount commissions. And the internet has added a whole new dimension to the brokerage business. It has taken a while to shake out but now there are essentially three types of brokers.

First is the full line broker, like Merrill Lynch, that provides full services and charges a full fee. They may negotiate a lower commission with a savvy investor but generally they have a fixed schedule within their firm. Typically this will cost an investor 3% or so on each side of a trade. So, if you sell 1000 shares of a $10 stock or a total market value of $10,000 when you sell you will net only $9,700 after commissions. And if you turn around and reinvest you will have reinvested (forgetting any taxes you may have to pay) only $9,400. That investment will have to go up nearly 8% just to break even, considering costs of selling that investment down the road. Do many of these trades and unless you are having a very good run in the market you will see your capital shrink.

The second type of broker is the discount broker that still offers some services. Schwab, TD Ameritrade, and Fidelity are some of the better known. For those who qualify USAA is also one of the better ones. They offer a far lower commission than the traditional full line broker and they offer somewhat less service. They will provide some information but little advice on what investments you should make. That is full line service. But at the discounter you will pay maybe half or less what the full line broker charges.

If you are making your own decisions it is foolish to pay full line services. You are paying for something you are not getting – advice and hand holding. Not only that but brokers being brokers the full line broker will likely call you frequently to induce you to make a trade with them. They may have the best of intentions, their commissions aside, but they can lead you astray from an investment plan that is well thought out. Most of the very good brokers do not handle small accounts. The really good ones move on quickly to manage large sums, usually through mutual funds or hedge funds. What you and I are likely to get at our typical broker is a pleasant, well-meaning broker who may know less than you do about investing. That can be more of a hindrance than a help to your investment plan.

Finally there is a broker that I use most frequently. The deep discount broker. They provide only one thing, execution of your order. For that you pay about 3 cents or less a share in commissions. At Muriel Siebert I pay a flat $14.95 a trade for on line trades. At Ameriprise (formerly American Express) I went with them when the waived annual fees on IRA's for life and for holding $25,000 or more in an account gave you three free stock purchases (except for a $6 transaction fee) a month and sales were $24.95. Holding more than $100,000 and you got 10 free trades a month, buys or sells. I used to keep an individual account with them but when they introduced a monthly fee for accounts of less than $500,000 I moved that business to Muriel Siebert who has no such fee.

Brokers can also nickel and dime you with fees for IRA accounts, inactivity fees, monthly fees for accounts under a certain amount, etc.

If you have a sizeable account that you are trading you may find that a full line or discount broker will be willing to negotiate a commission with you similar to a deep discounter. If so this can be an advantage, especially if the broker is in the same city with you. The convenience of having someone who you can talk to in person, should the need arise, and an office you can walk in can be worth something to you. Perhaps. What it is not worth is paying much more than the deep discount commission, unless you are using them for information and advice.

In choosing a broker you need to first decide on the level of service that you need. Frankly, if you need more than execution you should probably consider using a good no load open end mutual fund family and avoid a broker all together. Vanguard and Fidelity are probably two of the better fund families. Some discount brokers allow you to buy these funds at no cost unless you get in and out in a 90 day period. This can be a great convenience and is well worth considering. We will discuss no load mutual funds later. Let me say here that you should never buy an open end mutual fund with a load through a broker (or ever for that matter) as there are plenty of good no load funds. Buying a load fund through a broker you will be paying 4 to 7% of your capital for nothing but their doing the paperwork for you. Study after study has proved that so-called load mutual funds (those that brokers will sell you) do not perform any better than their no load brother/sister funds that have no commission.

Once you have decided on a broker you need to be sure that they will handle your trades efficiently. That may be where a local broker can be handy but in many years of internet trades I have found that to be more than satisfactory. If the local broker insists on providing unwanted advice then look elsewhere. From my experience it is just as easy to work with New York as it is locally.

One further word on brokers. It is good to let them hold all stock certificates for you in street name. Just be sure you elect a cash account (not a margin account) with them so they cannot loan out your stock to short sellers. This is a great convenience and in event of loss of a stock certificate can save you a great deal of trouble and cost. If you keep stock certificates and lose one you will end up paying 10% of the face value for an insurance bond before a new certificate will be issued. Losing a certificate can be very costly and until replaced you cannot trade the security. You are much better leaving stock certificates in street name with your broker.

A good broker, with whom you develop a comfortable and personal relationship can be a big help in your investing. You may even be willing to pay them a few extra cents a share than the deep discounter just for their personal attention. You have to weigh the benefits and costs. Just remember that commissions, like taxes and inflation, eat into your capital. They reduce your gains and increase your losses. Keeping commissions and other costs as low as possible can be the difference between profit and loss in some cases or can permit you to make trades for small price moves where a higher commission would make such trades impossible.

We will cover later an arbitrage technique for closed end mutual funds. You need a very low commission to make this work. But, as I do, you may want to pay more than the bottom end commission if your broker can assist you in making arbitrage work for you.

In my account the difference in execution of even $1/8^{th}$ of a point can make the extra commission worthwhile. For example say you are planning to sell 10,000 shares of a closed end fund at $10 a share and immediately turn around and buy 5,000 shares of another closed end fund (typically trading at a higher discount to net asset value) at a price of $20 a share. For this example assume no taxes are payable on the sale. Your gross proceeds would be $100,000 less commission. If the commission were 3 cents a share the commission would be $300 leaving you with $99,700 to reinvest. Since the cost of the new closed end fund would be $100,000 you will need to add $450 to do the transaction since you will have to pay $150 commission at 3 cents a share on the purchase of the 5000 shares of the new closed end fund. Let's assume that you only have to pay a commission of 1%. In this case $1000 ($500 on each side of the transaction) to do the trades. But if your broker were able to do these trades for you and save you $1/8^{th}$ of a point on the sale and another $1/8^{th}$ of a point on the purchase what has the broker done for you. Saved you $1,875. So instead of costing you more, paying the 1% and paying more commission actually saved you money. Of course this is hypothetical and it all depends on whether the broker can actually do this for you.

In this example you are actually $1,275 ahead by paying the broker more to watch your execution and assist you in achieving your price point. True, with a deep discount broker you could have placed a limit order and perhaps achieved this same result. But it is not likely that they can provide the level of service that you need to make these kinds of trades, especially if the amounts involved are substantial. And with a limit if you place an "all or none" limit your trade may not get done. But if you do not place all or none you could find only a few shares get traded for you and if all not done in one trading day you will end up paying more. Or if you change your limit before all trades are done the same may happen. With very large capitalization stocks all or none works fine but with other than very large caps (like GE, Microsoft etc.) this can be tricky. We will discuss this in more detail later but for now my point is that sometimes (not very often, but sometimes) using a broker and paying somewhat more than a deep discount price can be useful.

If you are simply selling a few shares of stock to pay taxes or to withdraw funds and you are not engaged in an arbitrage technique like the one above, then you should always use the deep discount fee structure. Especially if you plan to place a market order. Market orders are quite cheap for a broker to execute when compared to limit orders and you are not likely to get better execution from your local broker than a deep discounter in this transaction. Likewise if you are making a purchase using a market order you should not pay more than deep discounted commissions.

A word on market vs. limit orders. Both can work and both can present problems especially in smaller companies or in fast moving markets. I have seen cases where placing a market order to buy or sell has been a disaster in thin or fast moving markets. These are best placed in normal markets and stocks with larger capitalizations. You never want to do this for a pink sheet company or a small capitalization company especially if shares you are buying or selling are substantial. With limit orders you can find that this too is a problem in these stocks. If part of the order is executed one day and other parts on other days the ultimate commission can be much higher and with changing market conditions you may find that you end up buying or selling fewer shares than you wanted. If you change the limit with a deep discounter you will find that the commission structure changes.

You may find that you want two or more brokerage accounts. Spreading your investments over two or three brokers can have an advantage provided that you are not increasing the cost of holding your securities (e.g., inactivity fees etc.). If there is a problem with one of your accounts you will not have all your investments locked up until you straighten out the issue. You may want a full service brokerage account for securities that require a full service broker and one or more discount brokers. I currently use a full service broker and two deep discounters. That has worked well for me.

A little time spent learning about brokers and commissions will be time well spent. When new services come out or changes in the terms of your agreement with your broker changes be sure to check them out. You will give yourself a distinct edge in your investing if you can reduce your commissions to a minimum.

CHAPTER SEVEN. DESIGN OF YOUR PERSONAL INVESTMENT PROGRAM

INTRODUCTION:

You probably thought we would never get here, to a discussion of how you should set up and handle your own personal investments! Hopefully by the time you finish this book you will understand that it is necessary to lay the foundation before we begin to build the specific structure of your investment plan.

Now I may frustrate some of you as I outline what to me is a sensible investment plan in that I am NOT going to give you specifics of funds or stocks. I do this for several reasons. First, you have to learn to do your own research and make your own decisions. Second, if I include specifics here by the time you read this those ideas may no longer make sense. True if I give you examples it may help to clarify the procedure but if I do that I fear it may lead you to conclude those are not examples but something to follow. So after giving this a lot of thought I have decided to give you the principles, sources to do your work and then let you decide what is best for your situation.

The principles that I espouse here may not be easy to absorb at first. They differ from the conventional wisdom on Wall Street and must be thought through with some care. Only if you understand completely the concepts involved can you hope to implement them successfully. Part of the reason for my writing this book is to set out for myself in one place the specifics of my program so that I can refer back to it from time to time to be sure I am not deviating from my own advice.

Believe me it is easy to deviate! Read the Wall Street Journal or Investors Business Daily or watch CNBC or follow any number of newsletters and you will see how easy it is to ride an emotional roller coaster in the investment world. There is seldom a time you cannot find three opinions being espoused by equally credible investment advisors. Some will urge you to stay out the market, others will advise you to be fully invested and a third camp will be in between. The electronic broadcasters, be it CNBC, Fox Business or Bloomberg, all try to give a "balanced" approach which means you will likely be getting all three of these at the same time. Each camp can make a plausible case for its position. But obviously only one of the three can be right! Markets either go up, down or stay relatively constant.

Sometimes particular parts of the market will move against the trend and obviously on even the darkest days some stocks go up and on sunny days some stocks will go down. So to be a successful investor you must develop and stick to a plan for your investments. That plan will change from time to time but you should make changes carefully and with a great deal of thought. Never make changes while in a high state of emotion because of either giant up or down moves in the market. Emotion you cannot avoid but you can control how you handle it.

So with this preface we begin on developing your personal investment plan, putting into practice some of what we have covered above and discussing some subjects in greater depth than before.

We will begin the "cash reservoir system" which is the need to maintain a cash reservoir to protect against unexpected needs and against down years in the market. A properly designed reservoir will let you sleep comfortably at night and will keep your investment program intact. We have previously discussed this concept in thumbnail fashion but now we will get into specifics.

7.1 CASH RESERVOIR FOR DOWN YEARS

No matter how savvy you are as an investor you will miss a turn or two in the markets or you will decide to ride out a correction to protect your tax position or for other reasons. Sometimes the correction is so violent that you cannot anticipate it. In order to protect your needs for cash during such periods you need to design a reservoir of cash to meet a variety of possible needs.

This reservoir allows your investment fund to rise and fall with market conditions which sometimes, like in October 1929, October 1987 or in 2008, occur with considerable violence. The purpose of the reservoir is to keep a fund constantly available that will level out the ups and downs of the market. Like a reservoir created by damming up a river. In the case of a river the reservoir fills up when the stream flowing into it is at a peak. At the other end of the reservoir a relatively constant flow is kept moving down stream.

Water reservoirs serve many purposes. They control floods, provide hydroelectric power and provide water to send downstream in times of drought. Our cash reservoir serves a similar purpose. By keeping our withdrawals from the cash fund relatively constant we are not tempted in good times to spend money that will be needed in bad times. It is so easy in good market years to spend part of that year's excess without realizing that part must be put aside for the leaner years. So in the good years the reservoir must be allowed to fill so that in down years enough will remain to see us through to the next good year.

This concept is especially important for retired people or people that live off all or part of their investments. Especially in times of inflation it is too easy to end up spending part of your capital fund unless you have a disciplined method for withdrawing only that portion which is income in excess of taxes and inflation. Keeping two separate funds, one a cash reservoir and the other your investment fund, may help to prevent you from spending part of your capital.

As we discussed earlier just how much cash is needed and in what form should it be kept is very personal to your own situation. And you will find that through various stages of your life the size of the reservoir will constantly change.

If you have a good and stable job that pays a consistent income your need for a larger cash reservoir will be less than a retiree that is living exclusively from investments. Most of us will be somewhere in between.

There is another purpose for the cash reservoir. It allows us to be aggressive, as we should be, in our investment fund without having to allocate that fund to try and protect for our emergency needs. Most allocation strategies attempt to protect your investment fund. In my strategy you protect your investment fund by aggressively investing the fund while providing for emergencies and day to day needs through your cash fund. Knowing that you will have sufficient cash for your expected needs frees you to look to the really long term in your investment account. You do not need to keep tinkering with your investment account to protect it against possible withdrawal needs if those needs are taken care of by your cash reservoir.

Your cash reservoir may contain some investments similar to those in your investment account. But these will need to be tightly controlled to protect your cash reservoir. For example, if you are in an environment of low interest rates (as we have been since 2008 and the Federal Reserve estimates will continue into 2015) you may have a part of the reservoir invested in utility or other dividend paying stocks. But these need to be limited to protect those investments against market declines and your reservoir will need to be larger just to protect against declines in these investments.

One approach you may consider is a dumbbell approach. Keep say 75% of your cash in FDIC protected or EE bond investments and the remaining 25% invest for high yield spreading the risk among various high yield classifications. Even if you are getting nearly zero on your 75% you may be able to attain a 5% or better yield by using 15% or higher REIT or other investments in the high yield category. Just be aware that this is a risk and you are taking it to try to maintain a reasonable rate of return in an unusual market. And when rates begin to rise you will have to act decisively and quickly to prevent losses in that 25% position which will be vulnerable to rate increases.

You should never mix or confuse your cash and your investment accounts. In your cash fund you are protecting your current needs. You cannot allow an investment to reduce the fund below its safety level. On the other hand you could see your investment account decline by 50% and know that you can wait out the next move upward. Hopefully you will not often suffer such a loss but is likely that you will find yourself having to ride out a correction or a bear market. What you cannot do is to allow your cash fund to erode below its safe level. It is fine to invest part of your cash fund as long as you keep firmly in mind the purpose of this fund and take the steps needed to protect it in the event the market moves against you.

At the current time I am trying to keep three years' worth of cash in my own reservoir. There is no magic in the three years, it could be two or four. I try not to be overly conservative in my cash fund, using the dumbbell approach described above, since I know that what I keep in this fund limits my overall investment performance. It is a tradeoff that has to constantly be reviewed.

The form in which I keep this cash depends on current tax policies. I keep in mind my anticipated taxable income and taxes to be paid for the next couple of years watching interest rates and whether those are trending up or down. Obviously if interest rates are rising rapidly and my opinion is that they will continue to do so I will not want my cash fund tied up in longer term bonds or longer term CD's. Likewise in a falling interest rate environment I may want to be in longer term bonds or CD's. When rates are relatively low then I may want to put a part of the fund in stock investments if their total return (dividends plus capital appreciation) appears attractive.

As we discussed in an earlier section you should consider various forms of tax free investments for part of your cash fund. A part of this fund might be in Series EE savings bonds for example. For many years investment advisors would have laughed at using Series EE bonds. But the last laugh could be yours today. If you buy EE bonds and defer taxes on any build up in value today you have two advantages. First, you can keep these bonds for many years before having to cash them in. There may also be tax advantages and at times variable rates. As the taxable income builds without any tax being paid and if you have a serious problem that affects your income for a particular year you can then cash in the bonds with the income being taxed at very low rates. Taking out multiple bonds (e.g., in $100 or $1000 denominations) lets you cash in some but not all at one time therefore letting you determine the amount of taxable income to take down if you need to sell. So, if you lose your job and are out of work for a year while in transition to the next phase of your life, this may be the time to take down the EE bonds from your cash reservoir.

Other investments can be used as part of your cash reservoir too. If you have a 401(k) plan at work that allows withdrawals in an emergency that may be something to use for part of your cash reservoir. The Roth IRA permits you to withdraw contributions without penalty although the drawback is you cannot put that money back in once it is taken out. Still it can form part of your emergency plan.

Of course some of the cash fund needs to be available on a moment's notice without having to incur penalties or large adverse tax consequences. Therefore, you would never rely solely on EE bonds or on other than FDIC protected accounts. But these less liquid assets might form a base of your emergency account. Let's say you decide to keep a 3 year cushion in your cash reservoir. And assume this means you need $150,000 in this fund. You might keep $50,000 in EE bonds, $50,000 in a Roth or other accessible tax advantaged account and the remainder in an FDIC protected checking account.

There is no magic in this allocation. I will not try to give advice on how much you need to keep or how best to keep it. That is a very personal decision, depending in part on your psychological makeup, your work and personal situation as well as on economic conditions. And those will change over time.

In setting up your cash reservoir you should start by deciding how much to set aside, keeping in mind the discussion above. You need to put away the minimum amount that lets you sleep well at night even if your investment fund were cut in half or worse. Remember in the Great Depression stocks on average declined 90% eventually.

Once you have decided how much to set aside you next need to decide how best to put those funds to work so they are not sitting idle but are producing some return. You should, at a minimum, plan to at least break even on your cash fund on an after tax, after inflation basis. This may mean using tax free income investments for part of the fund, some high yield bonds or stocks and some dividend paying stocks.

Only when you have set aside the cash reservoir should you consider making true investments. It may take younger investors a number of years to fill their cash reservoir. It is hoped that they will use Roth and other IRA accounts as part of this reservoir, hoping they never really have to touch them until retirement, if then. In my opinion you should not try to invest until you have set aside your cash needs in a reservoir, only then can you be truly free to aggressively pursue your investments to make a meaningful return that is worth your effort and risk.

Assuming you have created and filled your cash reservoir, we now turn our attention to the remainder of your investment assets and discuss how to approach your investment funds.

7.2 INVESTMENT FUND – IRA AND OTHER TAX DEFERRED INVESTING

The first part of your investment fund should go into a tax deferred IRA starting with a Roth IRA to extent you are permitted to contribute to the Roth. We have discussed briefly above the advantages that these funds can have and how much leverage they can give you in your investment program. True, these moneys are not available for your immediate need without paying taxes or incurring penalties (with some exceptions) except for a Roth IRA, but in most cases the rewards over time far outweigh what you may give up in the present.

To show you once again how powerful these tax deferred investments can be we will consider two examples. First is a taxable investment fund with an average annual earnings rate of 10% with a comparison of an IRA investment fund earning the same 10%. We will assume a starting fund of $10,000 with no further investment, inflation at 5% and taxes at 33% applicable to the taxable investment fund. Results: after inflation and taxes after 30 years (an investor 35 to age 65) is $174,494 before deducting for inflation. After inflation the result is $38,338. In the taxable fund the result would be $16,419 after deducting taxes. Advantage IRA by $21,969 but of course if the IRA is not a Roth it will ultimately be taxes on withdrawal. This is for a one time investment by someone at age 35 holding until age 65. If that investor now withdraws this fund over a period of 20 years (age 65 to 85) the result in an IRA is withdrawal the first year after inflation is removed amounts to $8,596 and remains relatively constant after inflation assuming still a 10% investment return during the period of withdrawal. At the end the fund has reached zero and the last year withdrawal is $6,716. Obviously the taxable fund would result in much lower annual rates of withdrawal.

But this is not the real power of the IRA investment. If we consider that the investor is successful in reaching the 25% annual return, with all other assumptions the same, then at the end of the 30 year period the fund with only a one time investment of $10,000 reaches $1,777,145 in an IRA but only $273,849 in a taxable account. Note that the results are nothing short of spectacular comparing the IRA and the taxable account. Yes, I realize that most of us will not reach the level of 25% a year compounded but this does show how powerful reaching for that target can be.

Also remember this was for a one time investment of $10,000 while most of us will be contributing on a regular basis throughout our working lives and the results of doing that are significant. For example, assume at age 35 you contribute $10,000 each year until you are 65. And use the 10% annual return and 5% inflation. We already know that the taxable account will result in much lower totals at the end so we will focus only on an IRA account. The after inflation value on this account at the end of 30 years will be $980,602. And remember this is in current dollars. True on withdrawal taxes will be due (unless in a Roth IRA) but this is certainly a nice retirement fund. If your employer matches your contributions your out of pocket cost of contributions will be lower.

Of course if you start at an earlier age then the end result is much larger. If for example you have children who work during high school and college and they can contribute to a Roth IRA the results for them later in life can be significant. You may want to consider letting them contribute to a Roth IRA and you make a gift to them of an amount equal to what they put in the Roth.

Convinced of the power of tax deferred investing? I certainly hope so. The results from tax deferred investing under current tax laws is compelling. It is really tough to make money on your money outside of a tax deferred investment account if you take inflation and taxes into account. About the best hope an individual investor has is to make use of a Roth, Traditional IRA, 401(k) or other tax deferred account and go for as large a rate of return as possible with an aggressive investment plan. Not gambling, not foolish investing but nevertheless investments with potential for major growth of capital. Current high capital gains taxes (about to go much higher apparently) make staying ahead with a taxable investment fund extremely difficult.

Once you have set aside a sufficient cash reservoir the next step is to set up your IRA. First make maximum use of the Roth IRA (except perhaps an employer Roth 401(k) which generally if you are in high tax brackets is not a good choice over the traditional 401(k). You are limited in contributions to the Roth as income rises but take as much advantage of this as you can. Unless you are using this as part of your cash reservoir then invest this fund aggressively as we will be suggesting shortly. Because you can withdraw your contributions to the Roth IRA at any time without a tax penalty it can in early years be an excellent part of your cash reservoir. Of course since it cannot be replaced once taken out you want to try to avoid doing this but it is there in case of emergency. You cannot until 59 ½ withdraw any accumulated gains on the account without incurring a penalty but your contributions can be withdrawn with no penalty. In early years of a career you may also get a bonus in the form of a tax credit for your contributions depending on your income. You definitely want to take advantage of that bonus!

Even with the Roth you may have the chance to set up a 401(k) or its equivalent for self employed or those in 403(b) plans and these may be matched by an employer. If so you want to take maximum advantage of that matching. As your income rises you may want to contribute even more as it will reduce your current taxes.

If you leave an employer you will have the chance to roll over your 401(k) into an IRA account and you will likely want to do that using a self directed account at a deep discount broker where you can invest in a wide range of good mutual funds without commission in many cases or you can buy ETF or individual stocks.

Another word on employer 401(k) plans. Some allow for investment in that company's stock. Generally you do not want to put too much in any one investment including your own company stock. A lot of folks at Enron learned that lesson as they lost all their savings in these accounts when Enron went bust. If you think your company stock is a great investment I would still urge you not to have more than 5 or 10% of your 401(k) in that stock. The rest should be spread among a variety of mutual funds providing you with diversification and opportunity for long term gain. Each plan has different funds available so in discussing investments in a 401(k) plan (or its equivalent) we will be discussing this in broad terms not specific funds.

And once you have made contributions do not take funds out before retirement except in the case of an absolute emergency. You cannot put them back and you will be subject to possible penalties and taxes you can otherwise avoid. But most important is you will lose out on the year after year accumulation and compounding that results in a satisfactory fund for your later life.

We have already discussed at length why you should "go for the gold" in your investments. In my opinion except in your emergency fund it is foolish to "play it safe" in your tax deferred investments. I can understand why bankers, insurance companies and others want you to go for "safe" investments that they offer. But from your standpoint the after inflation, after tax benefit from deferring use of your money is just not worth it unless you are achieving a minimum of 10% annual average growth. Is setting aside money at less than 10% really worth it? Not to me it is not. If that is the best I can do I would rather spend my money now and enjoy it before inflation and taxes eat it away.

That is just what the average American taxpayer is doing. The American taxpayer is not stupid. They may not know just how they are losing ground in the current economic environment but they "feel" the sense of loss. They know in their hearts that savings is not worth it…. sadly they are right!   Through inflation and taxes the saver in America is the loser. Spenders are rewarded in many ways and savers are penalized.

It does not take a genius to figure it out. Oh, the politicians think they are really clever and can put one over on the people, but they are not kidding anyone, except themselves. As the old saying wisely put it, you can fool some of the people some of the time but you can't fool all the people all of the time. It takes a while for people to realize that their savings are being wasted and stolen. Once they realize it they are not about to let it happen again.

Two points about the current political climate are worth noting as the climate affects investors. First, Congress changes the rules continuously, making financial planning very difficult if not impossible when looking out over long periods of time. Planning more than one session of Congress at a time is dangerous. Without a second's thought Congress will change rules on which people have relied and planned and will destroy those plans. Second, the current Congress has placed severe penalties on savings and investment. The average American is better off being nearly poor than nearly rich. If you are nearly poor you will get free college education for your children, medical care will be paid for and your old age will be supported, all from government tax funds. If you are nearly rich you will find your assets constantly under attack from inflation and taxes. If you are truly rich (in 2013 an asset base of $10 million or more) you are ok and if you are poor you have a burden that is difficult but at least there are safety nets to cushion your fall. True there are holes in the net as our homeless and mentally ill make all too clear, but the fall for the poor is not nearly as hard as the fall for the nearly rich – or what we once called middle class.

It is my thesis that Congress is rapidly eliminating the middle class in America. True there are many other factors at play from robots to globalization. But the middle class more than the rich is where the money is for taxes and that is the class that for now bears the burden of paying for all the services and cost of government and that burden is eating away at this vanishing class. The truly rich are pampered by the politicians in order to gain contributors to their campaigns and achieve their one true goal --- reelection.

The poor and their supporters have led the middle class into thinking that all their problems can be solved by taxing the rich. What they don't tell the middle class is that there is not enough money in the truly rich to make a dent in the problem. If every penny of wealth of the truly rich were taken and given to the middle class and the poor all of the problems would remain. All that would be lost would be the incentive to succeed. With no hope of ever getting out of the middle class why would the middle and lower classes continue to strive and work beyond meeting their daily needs? Russia has found that out, Great Britain has found that out. We seem to be the only country left that has missed the point.

This has a direct impact on your investment plans. You must realize that your planning will have to change with each session of Congress and with each session of your

State legislature. The investment plan you adopt today will have to be modified as you move forward. My objective here is to point out to you the realities of the system that you will be investing in to have hope of achieving success. If you really want to get ahead you will have to constantly protect yourself and your investments.

In concluding this section remember that at the present time tax deferred investment vehicles offer you the greatest potential for your investment program. Make use of them as part of your cash reservoir and then as the base of your investment program. Only when you have maximized these should you begin investing in a taxable investment program.

The types of investments you use in your taxable investment fund will be the same ones you use in your tax deferred program. So the next section will have application to your tax deferred program as well as your taxable investments. One exception is while you are using tax deferred programs as part of your cash reservoir. During that time you will want to lower your annual earnings expectations and lower volatility of these funds. Again, keep in mind what you are doing with your cash reservoir. It is your protection against job loss, illness, damage or loss of your car needing replacement or other emergencies. You want to take only limited risk with these funds. You must be able to get to them quickly if needed.

Only when you have fully funded your cash reservoir should you start to invest in the manner the next sections will discuss.

We end this discussion with one more example. You have decided that you need to keep two years of protection in your cash reservoir and that two years in your case means you need a $80,000 reserve. You keep $10,000 in an interest earning FDIC account and another $30,000 in a short term government bond fund . This is one year of protection. Then perhaps you put $20,000 in Series EE bonds and another $20,000 in a Roth IRA. Now let us assume that you can set aside $10,000 a year for investments. This means that within two years you will have moved the Roth IRA out of your cash reservoir and made it a true investment fund. As a result you may have started to move the IRA out of a government bond fund investment into more aggressive stock mutual funds but with a mental stop that if they decline by 10% you will consider moving them back into government bonds.

This is only an example and is intended to show you the kind of thinking I would use if this were my cash reservoir. As I have pointed out before every situation is different and so the best I can do is give you some general guidelines hoping this will be enough to let you design your own plan.

We move now to what most of you have probably been waiting for. Assuming that you have money to invest --- above your cash needs ---- how specifically do you go about it to achieve the highest possible annual investment return.

7.3 YOUR INVESTMENT FUNDS – WHAT TO HOLD AND WHAT TO BUY

First a word of caution. What follows assumes you have some basic understanding of investment types from open and closed end mutual funds to ETF's and individual stocks. If you do not have that background then pick up from your library a basic book on investing before going much further. It will make this discussion much more meaningful.

You may feel at this point you want a simpler plan and if that is the case go back to the Foreword at the start of the book and in bold print a simple plan involving 5 Vanguard funds is discussed. But if you want to be more actively involved hoping for more than average returns then the rest of this section will be discussing the more active program.

You may have several investment funds and each will have special characteristics and considerations. We will consider each of these in turn. Before turning to your taxable fund we will discuss briefly some special investment considerations of your tax deferred funds.

If you have a Roth IRA then the first question is whether that is set up with a bank in FDIC protected funds or perhaps a mutual fund family or perhaps a broker. In the first instance you will have very limited investment options and likely you are doing this as part of your cash reservoir emergency fund. In the second instance you will have the option to move funds among various funds offered by the fund family. In my opinion one of the best of these (and lowest cost) is Vanguard but Fidelity is also good and has wide range of funds available to you. Same for a number of other fund companies. Finally if you have a self directed account with a broker hopefully it is one that does not charge you for maintaining the account and provides a range of no cost no load mutual funds you can buy without commission. And with a broker you can also buy individual stocks, ETF products, etc. So you will want a low cost broker that provides the services that you need.

The Roth IRA has major advantages in that it accumulates tax free and you can after 59 ½ withdraw even the profits on the account tax free. It has estate tax advantages as well. At least this is true as of the time I am writing this in 2013. Congress can change this or, as was the title of one of my books, " In God We Trust---Because We Cannot Trust Congress!" And the latest wrinkle is they want to limit the total amount that can be in IRA accounts after discovering the major use of this by Presidential candidate Mitt Romney in 2012. Thanks Mitt!

The Roth IRA has one disadvantage over the Traditional IRA or 401(k) plan and that is that any losses in the Roth are your losses whereas in tax deferred vehicles since no tax was paid on contributions (only when taken out) the government gets to share in any of your losses. So in considering investments for the Roth you will want to take a long view and perhaps a little more conservative view than with the Traditional IRA. For example, if you decide that you want to include some speculative stocks that have great potential but also could go bust you would probably rather put these in the tax deferred account than in the Roth. True, if they succeed the profits will be protected forever but if they fail you will bear the entire loss. They do not call them speculations because they are sure things!

Probably your best option with the Roth will be using no load mutual funds and if you can use a deep discount broker like USAA or Fidelity then this will open opportunity to invest in any number of different funds usually without commission or cost.

So what funds do you choose? There are all sorts of sources to track mutual fund performance and Morningstar is one of the best of these. Your local library will likely have a copy and you can use their on line service as well. http://www.morningstar.com/

You will want a mix of funds and generally you will want something like 50% domestic growth oriented funds, 25% international oriented funds and 25% balanced funds. In the domestic group I suggest of the 50% that 15% are large capitalization, 15% mid capitalization and 20% small capitalization which totals to 50%. These are usually divided into value and growth and I would suggest considering half in each. As for international I would put 10% in emerging growth and 25% in global outside the US. And I would put half of these in large capitalization oriented funds and the rest in small capitalization funds. While these are my thoughts on allocation you should choose an allocation you are comfortable with and which you think will give you long term appreciation in this tax free account.

I would suggest you not have more than ten mutual funds in your mix of funds. If you have an FDIC protected cash fund available I suggest you start with that and as you make your decision on fun allocation and specific funds moving funds from the FDIC cash account into the various mutual funds. Some brokers or funds do not have FDIC protected cash accounts but use money market accounts. Unfortunately as the Reserve Fund proved these are not as safe as FDIC protected funds. Hopefully the fund or broker you choose will have a safe vehicle for your cash not invested.

Another source of mutual fund advice is the American Association of Individual Investors or AAII www.aaii.com. They offer low cost annual subscription or you can take a lifetime subscription which is quite reasonable at the time I am writing this and it has not changed in the last few years in cost. Also this organization will have idea on individual speculative stocks you may want to consider as well as a wealth of investment and tax publications available to their members. They have an annual mutual fund guide that can be very useful. Also they cover ETF and other investments. I do not always agree with their advice or techniques but still find them very useful. A lifetime subscription to their major services is currently only $290 and well worth the investment. Or you can buy a one year for $29 or a four year including their Computerized Investing service for $99. For me the lifetime is the best buy. And no, I have nothing to do with AAII other than make use of their service. Once a year they also produce an excellent tax guide that you will likely find useful. For a husband and wife it is best to take the lifetime subscription in both names so the survivor will have access to this service for their lifetime.

One warning on mutual funds (open or closed ended) and that is not to try to buy the hottest fund of the last year. Everyone wants to find a Fidelity Magellan when it starts to perform just as they would love to have found Wal-mart or Berkshire Hathaway (Warren Buffet's highly successful company) when they were dirt cheap. Frankly you are better off buying a lottery ticket and we know what a lousy deal those are! What you want are funds that have a solid record over a long period of time. Preferably those whose style of investing fits the current and likely future market conditions. For example, a small cap fund is best bought at the bottom of a bear market with larger caps toward the end of a bull market. Balanced funds such as Oakmark Equity Income (OAKBX) can be an example of a solid core holding. Not a recommendation but an example of one that has done well for me over many years. Not a home run hitter but a solid part of a core portfolio.

There are many excellent fund companies. You want to try and find ones with lowest operating cost to you. I have already mentioned Vanguard as one fund company with an excellent track record in this regard. And no, again I have nothing to do with that company only have high respect for its achievements. But there are others you will discover also with excellent records and low costs. It will take educating yourself and that is one reason I have not tried to give specific funds or stocks for you to consider. This is one area where you will have to gain education and do a bit of work.

AAII and Hulbert, previously mentioned, may be excellent sources of information for you and help you to get a good start on winnowing out funds and for self directed IRA or taxable accounts stocks. Both have been around a long time with excellent track records. You could do worse that starting with these reasonably priced services.

The next account you are likely to have is a 401(k) or similar account through your employer. At such time as you leave that employer you will have the chance to move this through a roll over to a mutual fund family or to a self directed brokerage account. I favor the latter provided you are not paying any or an excessive fee to use the brokerage. This gives you the widest range of investment options. Now assuming you have not left your employment you will have available only those mutual funds that your employer makes available to you which may be extensive or narrow. Hopefully one of these will be an FDIC protected cash account in which you can move funds if you decide to keep part of your fund in cash either before you decide on your options or if you decide to hold funds if you foresee a bear market approaching.

You again will want a mix of mutual funds in your portfolio but I suggest you limit your choice to 5 to 10 funds to give you the best opportunity for success. And you want to diversify the types of funds that you use in a way similar to what was discussed with the Roth. Again Morningstar and AAII are excellent sources of information in choosing your funds. Also you can go to Yahoo Finance and putting in ticker symbols can chart various funds available to you, view their performance, holdings etc. I suggest you look at the charts all the way from 3 months to the maximum and perhaps compare various of these funds (in Yahoo you can do this for up to five funds). In fact you should bookmark the chart for the funds in your portfolio so you can from time to time check and compare how they are doing. Limited to five items to chart at a time you may have to create Charts A, B, C etc. Or if you have multiple portfolio's e.g., taxable, Roth, 401(k), etc. you may want to consider labeling these A-1, A-2, A-3, etc. One defect in Yahoo is it does not take capital gains distributions or income distributions into account so a fund that has made substantial distributions may show a worse performance than is actually the case. Also I have caught Yahoo in a number of errors so be careful about any figures they might give and double check. Under the performance tab you will see performance at various periods including the best and worst three year periods.

One comment on rollovers. You are best advised to roll over to a fund or broker and have the account transferred rather than withdrawing and redepositing. In this way you will not risk running afoul of the tax rules on roll over. You may have to move funds into a particular fund that the new fund or broker will have available or into cash before doing the roll over but either the fund or broker can usually advise you how best to accomplish this. It can be tricky so be careful.

If you also have a traditional IRA (or have rolled over your 401(k) into what will then become a traditional IRA) you will have a broader range of funds and if using a broker other options to invest available to you. With a self directed brokerage account you will be able to invest in individual stocks. Now is the time to perhaps include 5 to 10 speculative stocks that you think have great potential but I would never suggest you allocate more than 10% of your fund to these types of investments. One great advantage to this type account is that if you have a significant capital gain you can take that gain and protect your profits without any tax consequence at the time you do this. Of course if you have a loss you cannot deduct that loss but remember that no tax was paid on this account when money was invested in the account so to the extent of your tax bracket the government is sharing in your loss. Hopefully you do not have many of these but you are almost certain to have some in your investment career.

As for the rest of your investments you again need to decide on an allocation perhaps similar to what was discussed for the Roth above and choose the funds or stocks that you think can give you the best performance while also providing you with diversification which limits your risk.

A source of investing in smaller stocks that has had a very good track record over time is through www.aaii.com which has screens of various stocks you can consider. If you decide to try mimicking their techniques it will take work and you will be dealing with a number of illiquid stocks that can be tricky to buy and to sell, especially if you have a large portfolio. This is likely to be more work than the average busy professional has time to devote to investing. But if you are so inclined their techniques may let you approach the illusive 25% annual compounded return. The best time to start a portfolio of AAII stocks is at the bottom of a bear market. That is when small US stocks tend to outperform larger stocks and will be selling very, very cheap. Near tops of bull markets or after a large run up in stocks as we are seeing in October 2013 after the rise from 2009 these stocks are generally not your best bet although in 2013 they are outperforming mid and large capitalization stocks. But that does not mean I would be chasing them.

There are some categories of stocks that if you are in a self directed account you may want to consider. Chief among these are closed end mutual funds. These trade like stocks and were discussed earlier as to how they differ from open end mutual funds which are the kinds of funds most of you likely think of when you think of mutual finds. ETF's are somewhat similar to the closed end funds except that they generally issue shares or retire shares depending on purchase or sales of their ETF and generally trade close to their NAV or Net Asset Value which is the total value of all their holdings divided by the shares outstanding. The closed end funds issue a set amount of stock (which of course they can issue more of in new offerings often giving rights to purchase to existing holders) and those shares change hands between shareholders. You buy and sell them just like any other stock. A good source of information on these is from the trade association CEFA which can be found at www.cefa.com and on which you can create a portfolio of closed end funds you own or are interested in owning. See Chapter 9 for an example of a CEFA portfolio.

The closed end fund offers an opportunity to buy at a discount to the net asset value of the fund while the open end fund you buy or sell at its net asset value, usually at the end of the trading day you buy or sell. Sometimes this discount can be substantial. At the bottom of the 2008 bear market JRS, a Nuveen REIT fund, sold at a massive 40% discount although it currently sells at a premium. One thing you never want to do with a closed end fund is to pay a premium. And an absolute no no is to buy these in an initial public offering. Wait 6 months and you likely can buy at a discount.

I personally screen these funds looking for those selling at a 15% or more discount to their Net Asset Value which is like paying 85 cents for a dollar of assets. But, remember that the discount can widen or stay the same in which case you will not get an advantage over a similar open end mutual fund. But if you study funds in which you are invested or interested in investing in you will likely learn when these are bargains and when they are not. Premiums will generally shrink as the fund's performance improves and increase in down markets and with poor performance. Move into one of these funds at the right time and you have the chance to significantly increase performance as they perform as well as their open end counterparts and if the premium shrinks you get an added kick to your performance. Of course this can work the other way too so if you invest in these you have to watch them but you can do this by checking your portfolio on CEFA. You will want to avoid these funds when their discount is widening and only reconsider when the discount stabilizes at a lower level.

And you may find with closed end funds you can do a bit of arbitrage if two funds which have a past track record and future good prospects sell at different discounts. For example you might find that Adams Express is selling at a 15% discount but General American is selling at a 5% discount. If you own General American you might consider selling that fund and buying Adams. Now in point of fact Adams tends to sell regularly at a 15% discount so you may or may not get an advantage doing this. And the two funds do differ in their approach. But it always pays to see if there are arbitrage opportunities especially if your fund that you bought at a deep discount is now selling at a small discount or even a premium. And the advantage in a tax deferred account is you do not have to consider the tax effects as you would if owned in a taxable account. Just the transaction fees and whether a swap might put you in an advantageous position.

REITs are a special subclass of closed end funds. There are some open end REIT funds as well. While providing a flow of income these funds can help to limit volatility in a portfolio although I try to limit these to 10% of a portfolio. They can have a special benefit mentioned later in a taxable account as often many of these pay out a dividend that is partially a return of capital and therefore not all of the distribution will be currently taxable although you will have to reduce your tax basis of the shares by the amount of the return of capital. But this is a subject for taxable accounts. It does you no good in a tax deferred account.

You may be disappointed to find I am not picking stocks or funds for you. But while I can help you to put together your investment plan and then monitor your performance you will have to do some of the work of finding the right funds and stocks to fit your plan and your comfort level. I have given you some sources of good information including Morningstar, AAII and CEFA. At your library you will also have access likely to Value Line Investment Survey both the regular edition and the mid and small capitalization editions. Perhaps you will have access to S&P Outlook there as well and that will have individual stock suggestions. There is also a closed end fund publication similar to Value Line available from http://www.herzfeldresearch.com/

Before we leave the traditional IRA a word about conversions into Roth IRAs. This can be an advantage but has to be studied very carefully. You will often see articles urging you to consider this. Do so with care. The best time to do this is likely in a bear market. If the market has dropped 50% or more and you find that your IRA other than Roth is down this could be the best time to consider making a conversion at the lowest cost. And you do not have to do it all or nothing. Rules have relaxed as of 2013 but of course you will need to study this and the rules if and when the time comes to consider making the conversion. If successful you will have moved from a taxable on withdrawal account to one which has no mandatory withdrawals during lifetime and no taxation on accumulations. A very good thing if it can be done at a low cost in taxes. But often to get this tax benefit significant up front taxes are required to be paid and if that is the case it is often not worth doing the conversion. Another time to consider this is if you have a low income year such as during a period of unemployment or right after retirement. If your tax rate is then much lower this could be a good time to consider moving part or all of the traditional IRA into a Roth IRA. While there are all kinds of websites that try to help you make the decision to convert you have to be very careful to consider whether continuing to defer or paying tax now makes the most sense. Unfortunately in most cases you will be guessing what future tax rates will apply and change in personal circumstances in the future may make what seemed a sound decision on hindsight not such a great idea. So consider this with care but any time you get caught in a bear market always take a look at this and see if it makes sense in your personal circumstance. Note in case of unemployment I am not talking about taking the money out but in moving it to a Roth. There are special rules that give you a period of time (I believe it is currently 60 days) in which to withdraw funds and then put them back into an IRA without a penalty or losing the deferred status. But you have to be very, very careful not to push the limits on this or miss the deadline due to illness, a car accident, etc. Just your luck to have car wreck on the way to the bank to redeposit the funds! I suggest doing this only in a true emergency where you may have need for funds for a very short period of time that you will be able to put back well before the deadline. And if you can, avoid this at all times as it is too easy to make a mistake or miss a deadline!

The final category of investment fund will be your taxable investment fund. Provided you have established a sufficient cash reservoir and taken advantage of the Roth, 401(k) and other tax deferred funds you may then have funds available for a taxable investment fund. If so count yourself very lucky and decide how best to invest in this fund to maximize your returns.

First of all let us discuss situation where you have a loss. Each September it is a good time to see if you have a chance to take a tax loss that you under current tax law can apply to any gains and up to $3,000 or ordinary income with any excess carried over to the next tax year and beyond. You can either sell a loss security and then wait 31 days before repurchasing or more than 31 days before selling you can double up on that security and then after the 31 days sell the first position to take a loss. But beware the Wash Sale rule which prevents you from taking a loss if you buy or sell substantially the same security within 31 days before or after taking the loss. But if you happen to own bonds you can sell one bond and buy a bond of a different duration or a different company if a corporate bond. Other than commissions that is a no brainer! You are not taking the risk you take doing this with stocks. With mutual funds you can sell one fund and immediately buy or transfer funds into a similar fund and then after the 31 days transfer back again if you choose. But be careful if buying a mutual fund which imposes a penalty if you make a change within a certain period after buying it without commission (usually 90 days but need to check). One added warning is that you need to know if your broker or fund has established rules for what securities are sold if you are selling less than your entire position. In that case you will almost always want to use the identification method versus first in/first out (FIFO) or last in/first out (LIFO) or average cost methods. That way you can identify your highest cost shares to be sold and get the most bang for your buck or in this case your loss. And if you do this right you will not suffer an economic loss, only a tax loss. And it is perfectly legitimate. Of course you can find you sell and wait out the 31 days in cash and the security has gone up in value. In that case you may have lost out. That is why either doubling up if you can or switching to an equivalent (but not the same) security will limit this possibility. But except for bonds there is no entirely sure thing either doubling up or selling and repurchasing or even if moving from one mutual fund to another that is similar. But usually the tax advantage is well worth this risk.

I tend to favor owning individual securities rather than mutual funds in a taxable account. The reason is year end capital gain distributions. You want to avoid these if you can and it would be a rare event when you would want to buy into a mutual fund, open or closed, just before it is going to make a capital gains distribution (usually near year end) in a taxable account as you will end up paying tax on what may be no gain to you at all! Individual stocks do not have this problem. And it is not just mutual funds you need to be careful about. REIT's and BDC (Business Development Corporations) are required to distribute 90% of their taxable income each year. Some of this may be a return of capital which would not be taxed and some may be capital gains which at the moment is favorably taxed but Congress wants to eliminate this and by time you read this may have done so. The rest will be ordinary income. REITS and BDC's are not quite as tricky as mutual fund distributions but may adversely affect your year end tax planning and come September it is good to look ahead and plan for any distributions you may have to take into account.

There is one category of investment I would urge you to avoid but which unfortunately often makes the list of recommended investments and that is the master limited partnership. The shares of these investments are sold like stocks but beware, they are not stocks. Instead they are partnership interests. Often these are in resources like pipeline companies, oil and gas producers, timber firms, etc. They can appear to offer very enticing returns. And often they do. But if they operate in a variety of states come tax time you may find you have to file tax returns in all of those states! That can be very costly even if you do your own taxes! Even in states without an income tax like Texas, Montana or Alaska you will find there are very complicated issues to address in filing out your tax return and when you ultimately sell these securities. Worst of all most of these wait until the very last minute to get you the tax information you need to file so you may end up having to get an extension of your time to file. Unless you are extremely wealthy, in which case you are not likely reading this book, you are best advised never to invest in these master limited partnerships. So be very careful if you run into these. They look like stocks, sell like stocks but they are not stocks as we think of them.

As with any of your investment funds you will want to diversify your stocks. I suggest you own no fewer than ten individual stocks and no more than twenty with the exception of a portion of this account, perhaps 10%, that you devote to speculative stocks in which case you might own five or ten of these.

Depending on your age if you find you have a substantial capital gain that would result in substantial tax you will have to consider if facing a bear market if you want to sell and pay the tax or ride through the valley with your stocks. And if you are older and want to leave these stocks to your heirs you will want to consider holding on to stocks with large capital gains that will be (in the lingo of the tax man) stepped up in value on death. In most cases you will not likely incur an estate tax and if not then stepping up the value to then fair market value will be a giant windfall to your heirs. Of course this also means that you may have a very limited ability to achieve higher than average returns in your taxable investments. These trade offs can get complicated.

There may be a variety of opportunities for tax savings that are beyond the scope of this book. For example donating appreciated assets in a taxable or even an IRA account to charity. If you make substantial donations this is something to consider to lessen your taxes. But other than this brief mention this is a matter best studied if you handle your own taxes or discussing with your CPA or other tax advisor.

CHAPTER EIGHT: MAKING THE PROGRAM WORK

8.1 EMOTIONS AND INVESTING

You may consider yourself one who is very emotional or you may feel you are as cool as they come. But anyone who thinks that they will not be subject to the usual human emotions that often wreck an investment plan had best think again. We are all human no matter how professional we might feel we are. We are subject to feelings of fear or elation. And we can be swept up in the emotions of others. Who did not feel that they just had to buy a house in the early part of the 21st Century? Who did not feel they had to own the latest internet stock back in 1999? And who had the courage to step back into the market in 2009 after its gut wrenching decline into that year?

So don't think you are immune, especially if you watch TV news or read financial publications are just standing around talking to your co workers or friends at work or social events. You will be exposed to the emotions of others. This is when you need to understand your emotions. Some of my best decisions have been when I felt I just had to get back into the market more heavily but then thought about whether this was my reasoning or emotions taking hold. Likewise when Time magazine and the New York Times are calling the death of the stock market with big pictures of a bear devouring stockholders it is likely time to think that this could be a bottom of the market. Or when they picture a happy bull it is likely time to think a top is here or near.

One of the ways you can take emotion out of your investing is to decide that you will hold a certain percentage in cash like assets in each of your investment accounts and I have suggested 25%. Yes, this will limit your performance but it will also give you a fund from which to add to your equity positions in down markets. And if you adjust your portfolio twice a year in early May and early October you will take some cash off the table in years when you have had a good year and put cash back to work in equities in down years. If you are off by merely a percent or two you do not need to fiddle with your accounts. But if you are more than 5% off your target this is the time to reallocate. The same is true within your portfolio. If you have decided to keep 50% domestic equities and that is out of balance or if the subcategories of large, medium and small capitalization stocks is off by 5% or more then make those adjustments. In taxable accounts you may need to take into account the tax effects and while taxes should never rule your investment decisions it should be taken into account. In that case I would give more leeway in making adjustments.

Twice a year adjustment seems adequate to me and doing it more frequently may lead you to make too many adjustments. There may be times when you will violate the rules but just be sure it is sound thinking and not emotion that is causing you to do this.

Another edge you can give yourself in the emotional rollercoaster that the markets can give you is not to pick up the paper or go to the internet to check how you are doing too often. Stocks are volatile, sometimes to extremes, and you may find yourself spending far too much time worrying about ups and down and not spending the time on your business or with your family. If you have made sound judgments on your program let it work for you and do not let yourself be emotionally whipsawed by TV commentators, the internet or financial publications.

I am not saying to trash your electronics and go into the electronic wilderness but use common sense and do not let your investments govern you instead of you governing them. Twice a year to adjust and once a year to review your overall plan should be more than enough for most busy professionals. More than this is overdoing it. True there may be times when things go haywire and you want to see if there are opportunities. But those should be rare events.

I do suggest that once a week, usually on a weekend when markets are closed, you take a look at the SP 500 quarterly chart that will show you major trends in the market and may help you to decide that instead of 75-25% in the market you want to be 80-20 or 70-30%. You will find a sample of this chart in Section 9.2 and in the next section a link to this chart via internet. Frankly for most professionals and busy people I do not suggest that you try to time this more than that. Going to 50% invested or less is dangerous to your longer term success. That does not mean you may not move to more defensive types of mutual funds in your portfolio. Better that you do that than try to move from equities to cash. It is too easy to make a mistake or get in the habit of trying to market time. Also once a week I suggest you go to ECRI's main website and see what the economic conditions are in their opinion. You can find this at http://www.businesscycle.com/ Often they will be giving interviews or providing a white paper on issues of importance and these are often worthwhile listening to or reading. But always remember that the economy and markets often diverge. So use ECRI for a view of the economy and how that may or may not affect your stocks.

These two resources can help you to make sound decisions on the state of the market and underlying economy. Then once a year in early January go to the library and look at Value Line's annual chart of the DJIA and its projections and perhaps make a copy of that page in their Opinions pages. It will give you a polestar to focus on as you think of your investments.

I will discuss the SP500 quarterly chart and the ECRI in more detail in sections coming up but for now just know that in all probability these are the major tools you will use to guide your portfolio if you are not a professional investor but a busy professional or manager with little time for your investments.

While the objective of this book is to help you to design an investment plan that will be a success it is not intended to fool you into thinking it will be easy. Hopefully if you follow some of the suggestions here you can design a program that will take very little of your time but it will take some time and some work on your part to get the most out of your investment program. Hopefully by now you have seen that the rewards of doing this right are worth that effort.

8.2 KEEP AN EYE ON THE MARKETS

There is keeping an eye on markets and then there is overdoing it. I find most busy professionals may tend to try to follow the market too closely. Either that or they do not follow at all until a headline (or their quarterly statement) grabs their attention.

While I am not a day trader I do have time in retirement to stay abreast of the markets far more than I did when a busy professional. I find I have to be very careful not to over do this myself and get into the trap of watching every tick of the market. Of course there are times when I am trying to buy or sell that I do watch every tick of the market trying to find the opportune time to enter or exit a position.

So what is best. First, weekends are good times to do a once a week check of markets. I suggest you book mark four items. First is a chart of the SP 500 calculated on a quarterly basis. This is a chart I use to try to spot possible bear market conditions (the only time I really try to time a market) and to spot bottoms once a bear market has been underway for a year or year and a half (usual duration of a bear market). You can find this chart at Marketwatch and currently the link to that is: http://www.marketwatch.com/investing/index/SPX/charts?symb=SPX&time=20&startdate=1%2F4%2F1999&enddate=1%2F25%2F2013&freq=4&compidx=none&compind=none&comptemptext=Enter+Symbol%28s%29%3A&comp=&uf=16&ma=1&maval=40&lf=4&lf2=16&lf3=32&type=4&size=2&style=1013

If you flip ahead to Section 9.2 dealing with measuring your performance you will find examples of this chart.

There is no need to look at this more than once a week. Later I will show you the best way to use this chart.

Next you may want to look at a chart of the SP500 available on Yahoo. This too is a good chart to check once a week or if you are planning to change a position either buying or selling it can be useful. I suggest you look at the 3 month chart, then the 6 month and 1 year and then the 5 year and maximum. Simple clicks will take you through this. It will give you a feel for the market short and long term. Again we will look at this a bit later but for now here is the link. http://finance.yahoo.com/q/ta?s=^GSPC&t=3m&l=on&z=m&q=c&p=b%2Cm20%2Cp%2Cm200&a=fs%2Css%2Cf14%2Cm26-12-9&c=

Here is an example of what this chart looks like in October 2013:

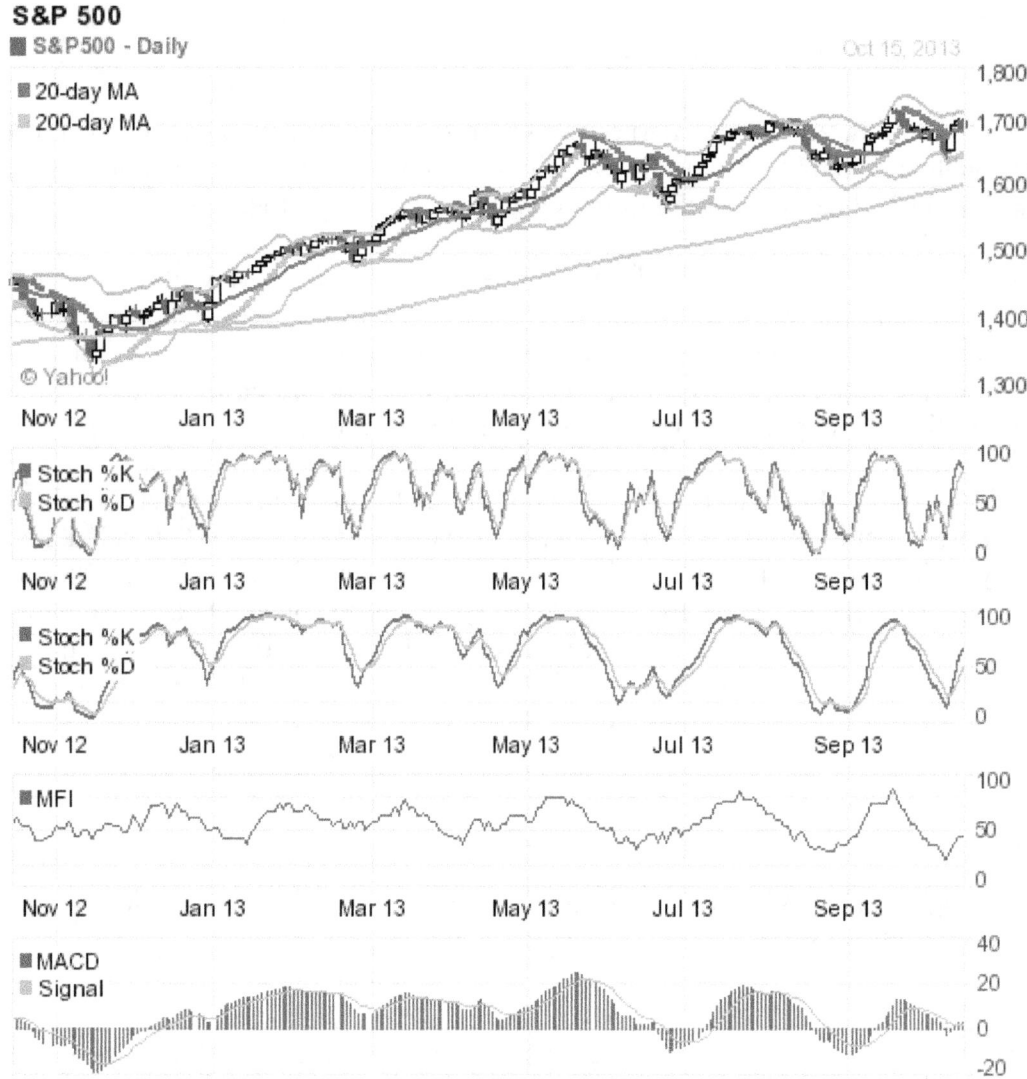

Note that I have not suggested that you check your own portfolio (as opposed to the market and economy) on a weekly basis. Frankly, for busy people I think once a quarter is more than sufficient and then especially at the two times a year that I recommend you consider reallocating- early May and early October. And you may find that no reallocation is needed. If so leave things alone, do not try to over tune your portfolio. Especially in a taxable account.

Finally there are two other sites to check weekly to get a feel for market conditions. One is Validea and can be found at this link currently. http://validea.com/stocks/mp.asp?tid=1&sid=2&pid=2 I set this to monthly reallocation and year to date although I occasionally will check last 12 months. This is an interesting site although I do not recommend it for finding stocks preferring AAII for this purpose. It will give you a rough idea of what areas of the market are doing well and how their portfolios are doing compared to the SP 500. It will also let you compare your own portfolio if you check on quarterly basis.

Finally there is the Closed End Fund site. Whether you own these or merely want to create a portfolio to watch it will show you how these funds are doing compared to the record of portfolios on Validea. http://www.cefa.com/ If you do not own funds currently then put in a few funds to watch and see how they are doing year to date and I suggest that you set this to year to date by NAV (Net Asset Value) and in descending order so the best are on top and worst on bottom. If you want to start with a simple group of stocks then I suggest the following list JSN, JCE,JRS, GAM, ADX,AWF, GHI, BME,PEO,GGN. These are not recommendations but will give you a broad spectrum to watch. JSN is a Nuveen broad index closed end fund. JCE is also Nuveen and is a modeled portfolio, JRS is Nuveen real estate trust. GAM and ADX are old line core funds. AWF and GHI are world bond funds with GHI focused on emerging markets, BME is Blackrock health sciences fund, PEO is old line natural resources fund focused on oil and GGN is a Gabelli gold and natural resources fund with about half or more in gold mining stocks. There are plenty of others I could suggest but this will give you a feel for YTD performance and the trend in their discount or premium to NAV.

If you bookmark these four sites it will not take you but a few minutes to get a feel for market conditions that will be affecting your portfolio. Shortly, as applied to your portfolio, we will discuss these in more detail.

8.3 STAY WITH YOUR PLAN

Probably the biggest mistake individual investors make is to sit in the quiet of their home and create a sensible plan for their investments. Then they read the headlines, listen to the news and watch their investments and let their emotions override their plan. They pull out of down markets in fear and buy into rich markets usually just when they are ready to top out. It takes discipline as well as an understanding of human nature (and your own emotional nature) to adopt a plan and stick to it. For some reason women seem better at this than men. But they also tend to be less aggressive in their investing so the two may trade off.

This does not mean that if you find your plan is not working that you should stick to it forever? Of course not. The days of the nifty fifty – buy these fifty stocks and hold them forever – has not worked for a very long time. But in and out day trading is not the answer either. Mutual funds that worked great for years can turn sour. For example, Peter Lynch was a terrific manager of the Fidelity Magellan fund for many years. He had a 29% compounded annual return for some 13 years. But the new managers have not had the luck or skill to repeat that success. Those that bought Berkshire Hathaway, Wal-mart, or other stocks that have skyrocketed in their early years or Fidelity Magellan in year 1 then they did well. Very well indeed! Many are multimillionaires if not billionaires. But what is your chance of hitting this jackpot? Likely you would be better off buying lottery tickets!

No you may not make my target 25% a year and probably will not. But if you adopt a sensible plan and thin out your losers and ride your winners year after year with maybe just a little bit of market timing it is likely you will do very, very well for yourself. And by market timing I am not suggesting going to 100% cash or 100% equities. I think for most busy people that the 75%/25% formula works best perhaps going to 80/20 if the SP500 chart suggest a bear market bottom and 70/30 or at most 60/40 if a bear market appears in prospect. And that requires nerves of steel. You WILL second guess yourself and your decisions. Especially in big down markets.

Another way to deal with down markets of the bear market variety (20% plus declines) is to move from positions that have held up to those that have not but ONLY when the bottom is in for that market. In that regard I suggest that the slow stochastic of the quarterly SP500 is an excellent gauge along with the fact that the bear market is a year to eighteen months in duration. If the slow stochastic moves below 20 and then the faster line crosses to the upside this has proved a very useful indicator of a bear market bottom. That is a good time to consider adjustments to your portfolio both in percent devoted to equities and within that portfolio with perhaps an emphasis on small capitalization stocks which do best off a bear market bottom. And be sure to use the twice a year rebalancing. It becomes of vital importance at this juncture.

With the 75%/25% plan in rising markets at times of your rebalancing you will be taking some of the chips off the table and storing them for the inevitable downturn. But this works ONLY if you stick to your plan. The same is true in spades in a bear market. There you will be deploying cash back to equities as the market falls as your percent in equities will fall with it. Yes, you will be catching a falling knife at times. But you will also be averaging down your costs.

And if you are in a traditional IRA at the bottom of a bear market, especially one as severe as 1973 or 2008, this is an excellent time to consider converting part or all of your traditional IRA to a Roth IRA. The key word here is "considering" as you still have to consider the immediate tax cost vs the ultimate tax cost when you reach the point of mandatory withdrawals. And if you are in a 401(k) of the traditional variety and can make a switch of that plan to a Roth 401(k) that could be the time to consider this as well. I am not a big fan of the Roth 401(k) for most people but this is an exception. Again, the key word is "considering" and it will depend on your age and time to retirement. The further away your retirement the less advantage to converting. If you are say 60 then this might make a great deal of sense.

In the quiet of a lull in the market or in a roaring bull market you will likely feel that you have your emotions in check and that you will not deviate from your plan due to emotions. I hope you are right, but likely you are not. Study after study of investors shows that stocks are one of the few items bought when expensive and sold when cheap.

I love to sail boats and perhaps a sailing analogy will be useful. Every sailor knows the feeling of exhilaration and fear that comes when a big wind is blowing and your boat is heeling with the sails barely skimming above the water. One wrong move and you are swimming instead of sailing. It is those times that your skill and knowledge as a sailor has to overcome your natural fears. You know that your keel is stable and that the harder the wind blows the more your boat will resist being capsized. But hanging over the side with your feet in the hiking straps and watching the sails get closer and closer to the water there is not a sailor in the world that has no fear at that point. But having recovered your boat time after time from this situation gives you confidence.

The same is true of your investment program. There will be times when your investment sails dip precariously close to the water, declines of 50% or more are not fun, believe me. And there will be times when you are sailing with a big wind at your back and your investment boat is flying down the water when you think nothing can go wrong. Any sailor that has sailed wing on wing (sails spread wide to each side with wind directly at your back) and then has the wind change radically and suddenly knows this is a prescription for a disaster of a jibe with the boom swinging like a baseball bat from side to side and any one standing may find suddenly they are swept overboard. In sailing, when the wind is at your back and you are going with the wind it is eerily quiet. Somewhat like riding in a hot air balloon gondola. The risk is at that point the greatest but you feel safer than when your boat is heeled over on a close reach into the wind or a beam reach which is the fastest point of sail. Analogies are always dangerous. But nevertheless they can make a point otherwise hard to put into words. You must, absolutely must put emotions aside in your investing and while it does not take watching your investments every minute of the day you do have to pay attention. And there are times you have to pay more attention than others. Anyone who tells you they have totally divorced emotions from their investing is fooling you and themselves. As an investor you have to understand you will have these emotions and learn to control them. It is not as easy as it sounds.

8.4 CHANGING CONDITIONS

Conditions and markets do change. You will have to adjust your plan as you proceed. Just as the investment plan that worked for my grandfather will not work for me, without adjustments, you will find your own plan will have to change over time.

We have already discussed checking and then reallocating your portfolio at least twice a year. One of those times, in a time that is calm and you feel rested and relaxed, go over your investment program in detail. Compare your results with those achieved by others who have long term plans. If you are falling behind, try to see why. If it is a temporary condition and you are convinced of the rightness of your plan then stick with it. If you see where improvements can be made then make a change. But do not make a change just for change's sake. But also do not be afraid to make a change if one is needed.

My number one rule in this regard is when in doubt do not make a change. Usually you are tempted to make a change because the investment you are in is temporarily out of favor. Making a change at that time can be a big mistake. Small stocks have times when they are in and out of favor. They tend to rise for a long period of time relative to blue chips and then undergo a long period of underperformance. The same is true of domestic versus international stocks. You need to make adjustments to capture the advantages of small stocks and avoid, if you can, the long periods of underperformance.

The one thing that is constant in the markets is change. Change in prices, change in types of investment vehicles, change in the underlying economy. The economist Schumpeter developed his analysis of capitalist economies with one central theme – creative destruction. By that he meant that there is a constant change and products that are on top one day are the next day's dogs, that by this process great capitalist changes occur. New products develop and old products are discarded. Any company or industry that thinks it is immune from this process is deluding itself. The buggy whip maker thought the automobile was a toy and a fad. The mechanical calculator maker disappeared when failing to understand the power of the computer chip. And on and on the process goes.

Some companies have created a culture that seeks to capitalize on such changes, others hold to what they have done in the past. The investor too must be involved in this process and understand the effect on their investment of creative destruction. One of the great problems is knowing who will succeed and profit from new developments. Dow Jones in the 1930's removed IBM from the Dow Industrial Average just when it was about to rise 3000%. A mistake? Maybe, but more than that it shows how even the most sophisticated investors can have difficulty in trying to guess where success will come from. A more recent example is Apple which went through a moribund period after its early computer success. Then came the I Pod, the I Pad and the I Phone. All phenomenal successes reflected in a stock price that started at $19 and soared. Now with Steve Jobs gone who knows. I believe that trying to find the IBM, Wal-mart or Apple of the future is a dangerous game for an investor. For every success there are hundreds if not thousands of failures.

If you are lucky enough to fall into one of these wonderful situations it will likely be because you are working for one of these companies or have a friend who does. I am not talking about illegal insider trading but merely understanding better by being on the ground what is happening than those thousands of miles away. But don't bet your investment program (or your 401(k)) on trying to hit the home run. For every Wal-mart there is an Enron or Lehman. If they come by luck then fine, but the search for these spectacular market success stories can take you away from an investment program that will make you far more successful. It is again the story of the tortoise and the hare. Fables continue from generation to generation because they have within them great kernels of truth. So too investment wisdom.

CHAPTER 9 KEEPING SCORE

INTRODUCTION

It is vital for your success in your investments that you keep a continuous tracking of how you are doing in relation to your goal. This is hard to do when you are adding to or withdrawing from your funds. The purpose of this chapter is to show you a couple of ways you might consider to keep track of your investments to help you decide if you are on or off track in your investments.

9.1 PERFORMANCE CHARTING

You will get brokerage statements or statements for your tax deferred accounts but they will not tell you all you need to know. What you need is to be able to compare your performance with a reference to see if you are on target or not. If you have a static portfolio this is pretty easy. You simply find the percentage increase or decrease for your various accounts and compare those with a major index, usually the Standard and Poor's 500 Index (SP500) for the same period. Or you can also check the Validea website. http://validea.com/stocks/mp.asp?tid=1&sid=2&pid=2 I suggest that you choose the following options: rebalance monthly, twenty stocks then the period you want to compare against e.g, year to date or last twelve months etc. Finally under investing style chose all styles. That will give you a broad picture. Note that the choices you make will NOT affect SP500 other than for the time period you chose to compare e.g., year to date, last twelve months, etc. If one of the styles of investing compares with the strategy you are using even better. You can compare your performance with that portfolio.

How often should you measure your performance? Probably for those not actively engaged with their investing doing this each of the two times you rebalance will work very well. That could be a time you might want to tweek your portfolios.

The problem with this approach is that not many investment portfolios do not have either additions or withdrawals or both. In that case it becomes much more difficult to make performance comparisons. While the method above is helpful it will not give you a very accurate picture of your relative performance. So once a year try to do a thorough analysis. First week of January is often a good time and you should record not only your portfolio performance but the SP500 for comparison. Another time that can make sense is September when preparing to do a reallocation in October. Whatever period you choose you will have to make some adjustments. First you will need to adjust the SP500 for inflation. To do that you can use the BLS website that lets you adjust for inflation using the government's cost of living figures. While this is not perfect it is easiest to use. http://www.bls.gov/data/inflation_calculator.htm Assuming you are doing this first of the calendar year you will enter the SP500 close on the last trading day of the previous year. For the end of 2011 that figure was 1257.60. You then input the year of 2012 (just following end of year 2011 for which the SP500 was entered) and then search for what the buying power figure is for 2011. Result is 1232.10. In other words you needed 1257 at the end of 2011 to have same buying power as 1232 gave you at the start of that year.

As for your portfolio you need to make the same adjustment to see how much value your portfolio lost (we are ignoring the rare event of a deflation) during the year due to inflation. Except for taxable accounts including your cash reserve in taxable accounts we are ignoring taxes and if you did not take money out of those accounts to pay taxes you need make no adjustment. I suggest that you come up with a total for each of your separate investment accounts.

Now you may want something called semi log graph paper. You can find this on line at no charge at the moment at http://customgraph.com/piart.php?art=579 Or you can buy this at any good office supply outlet. This is simply paper, despite its imposing name, that from top to bottom has a scale where each doubling of the figure below is the same distance up and down. As you go up the page the next double is half the size of the one below. From right to left it is standard spacing which is why it is semi log and not fully logarithmic paper. So why use this semi log paper? You need to use this to determine if your performance is rising (hopefully) at a constant percentage.

Now that you have your semi log paper you first need to scale it for the SP500 using the first year adjusted for inflation you want as your starting point. Then each year you add the SP500 for that year (adjusted for inflation from the starting point or you can adjust it using the last adjusted figure and going out one year). This sounds complicated but once you have gotten used to doing it you will not find it a problem. By doing this you are creating a graph of the "real" or inflation adjusted SP500. It does not help you to know that the SP500 doubled in 10 years if during that time it lost 50% of its value to inflation.

I would ignore your cash reservoir for this purpose since you are not trying to hit a homerun or even a double with that fund. Yes, you will have to adjust that fund for inflation but you will know to do that based on what your needs could be for that fund. It is your protection against adverse life events as well as adverse markets. What you do want to compare is your investment funds. Now we run into a problem. If you are making additions or withdrawals from that account (not counting capital gains or losses in a tax deferred account where funds are not taken from the account) you have to make an adjustment and frankly I have not found a perfect way to do this. If you are in a traditional IRA account and have reached 70 and into mandatory withdrawals and you withdraw either at the start or end of a year then it is relatively easy for that account. If your account is a large one and the contributions or withdrawals are small, say less than 2%, you are probably best just ignoring them. Otherwise you will have to use your judgment as to the adjustments to make. There are just too many possible combinations to help you much with this calculation. Worst case ignore the change for the year knowing you will be somewhat over or under estimating your performance.

The next step is to do with your investment accounts what you did with the SP500 and that is use the BLS website to adjust for inflation. That way you are looking at your "real" or inflation adjusted portfolio and comparing that to the "real" or inflation adjusted SP500 portfolio. For now we are ignoring taxes since in a tax deferred account these are either put off or deferred forever as in a Roth IRA. Again you will have to remember to take into account your tax situation remembering the formula we started with and that is to find your true investment return you have to take the total percentage return less inflation and less taxes.

Once you have made adjustments then record each of your investment funds on the semi log graph paper. I suggest you note each one of them separately and then a total for all of your investment accounts.

Ok, now I know this is not all that easy! While I want to make this as easy as possible taking as little of your time as possible that only goes so far. There is work to be done. You have to pick your funds and stocks, you have to pay attention to changes that could require changes in your holdings and you will have to work at testing your performance at least once a year.

Back to our semi log paper. The first year you record will not tell you anything about your performance. But after that first year you will be able to draw a line from the previous years recordings and then the magic of the semi log kicks in. You will now be able to determine the percentage gain from the slope of that line and it will tell you how you are performing relative to the SP500 after inflation and how each of your portfolios (assuming more than one) is doing compared to the others. You can then take your target and determine the slope of the line that represents 10%, 15% and 25%. You can then overlay that on your lines to see how your performance compares and whether you are on or off target. Two years data will obviously tell you very little. Five, ten or more years will let you smooth out the ups and downs to see if the general trend is going as you want to achieve your target.

I wish this were easier but making it easy would not give you an accurate picture of your performance. You will have to work at this to make it work for you. I was tempted to include an example but I think that might tend to confuse you rather than help you in the process.

Whether or not you use the semi log graph paper do keep a list of the values of the SP500 at year end and for each of your portfolios. If you use semi log paper you can record this information on that paper including adjustments you made to reflect "real" inflation adjusted values. Even without semi log paper it is a simple calculation to see the percentage gain from year to year. What is more difficult without graph paper is to see the trend line that will smooth out ups and downs so you can calculate the trend in performance both for the SP500 and for your total of all your investment portfolios and then for each one of those.

9.2 OTHER WAYS OF KEEPING TRACK

If you are comfortable with a computer spreadsheet such as Excel from Microsoft Office you can create a spreadsheet with the SP500 and your various portfolios and can create graphs from that data. I do urge you to use the SP500 unadjusted and next to it its inflation adjusted value. And as you go from year to year you need to adjust each year based on the prior year adjustment. The same will be true of your investment portfolios. And depending on the program you are using on your computer you may be able to do this on a semi log basis. You will note that the SP500 quarterly chart that I have suggested you use for determining the state of the market especially at bottoms of bear markets has an option to use a logarithmic measure and you can go back and forth to see the differences. You can do the same thing you're your portfolios.

http://www.marketwatch.com/investing/index/SPX/charts?symb=SPX&time=20&startdate=1%2F4%2F1999&enddate=1%2F25%2F2013&freq=4&compidx=none&compind=none&comptemptext=Enter+Symbol%28s%29%3A&comp=&uf=16&ma=1&maval=40&lf=4&lf2=16&lf3=32&type=4&size=2&style=1013

Here is what the non logarithmic chart looks like as of October 2013

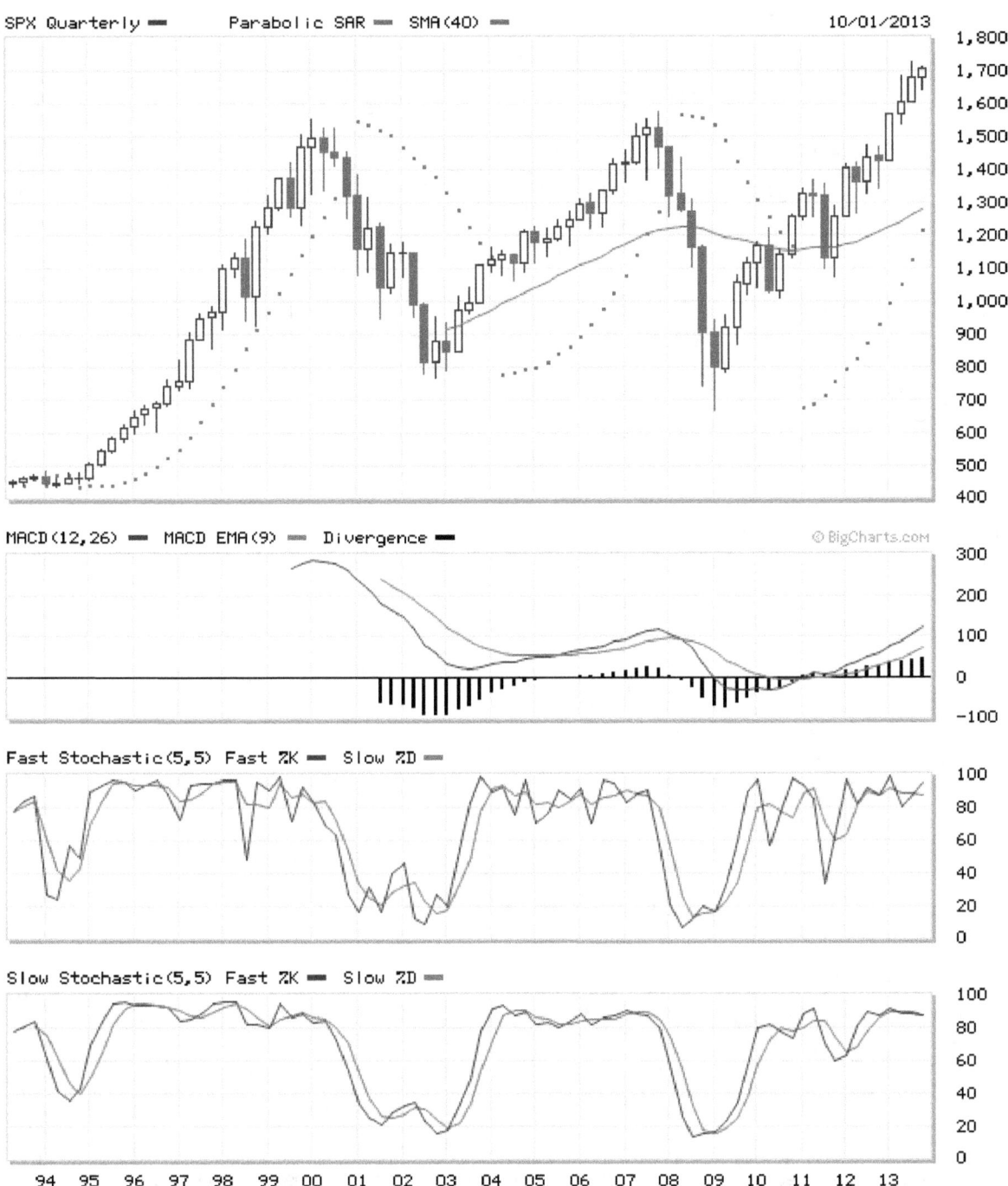

And now the logarithmic chart of the same data:

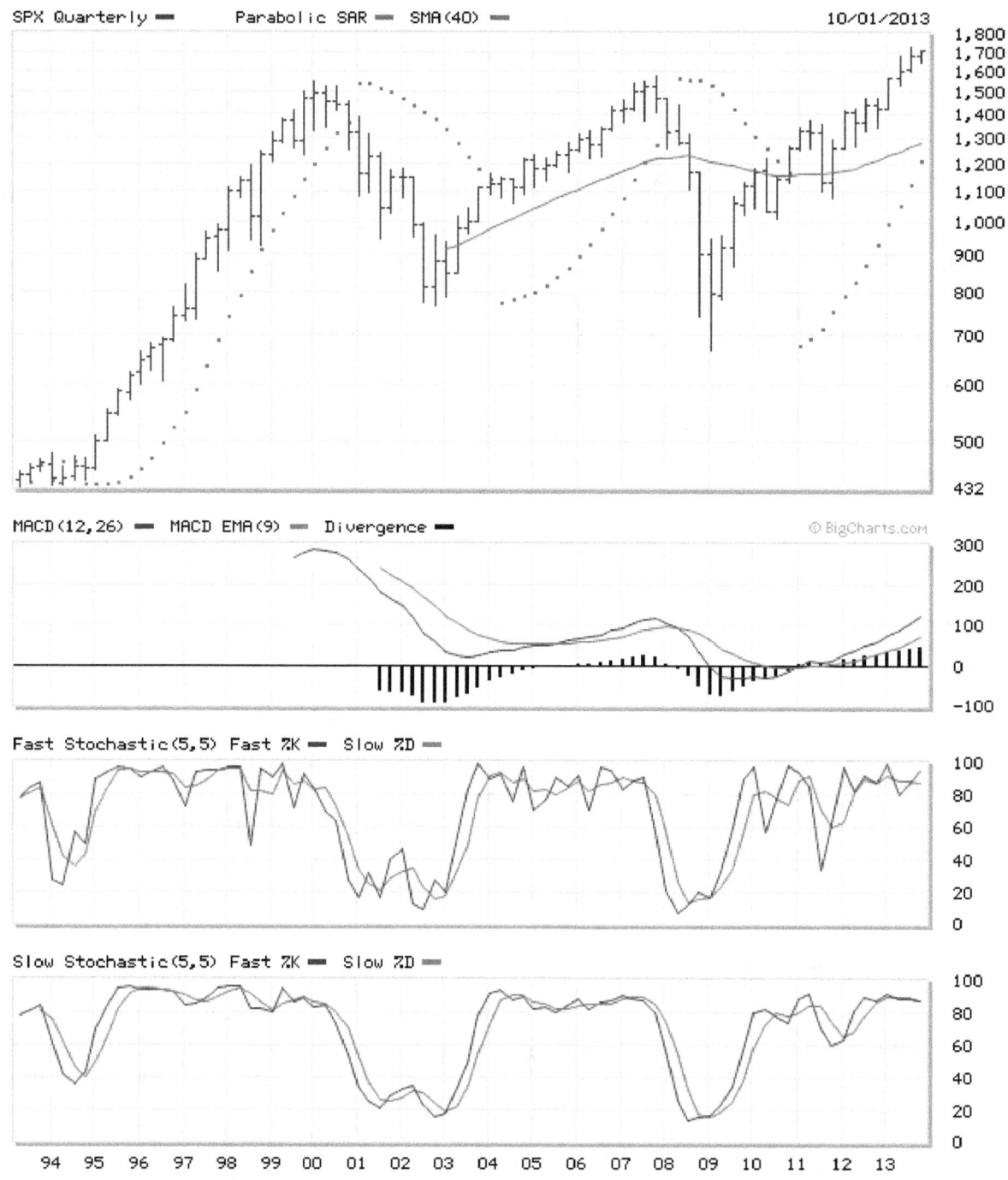

Note that only the top chart is logarithmic not the MACD, Fast or Slow Stochastic. To find the change go to display and change candlestick to logarithmic.

There are also any number of good computer services that will let you track your portfolio and do analysis. Membership in the American Association of Individual Investors will give you access to a number of these. http://www.aaii.com/ In addition to their regular service they have a computerized investing service that will have access to and discussions about a variety of tools used for monitoring and measuring your portfolio performance. As of October 2013 they still offer a one year membership for $29, a four year membership that includes four years of Computerized Investing for $99 or for $290 a lifetime subscription to both their basic service and Computerized Investing. Once again, I have no relationship with AAII other than being an admirer of their various products. The same is true of any company or service that I mention in this book.

CHAPTER 10 CONCLUDING THOUGHTS

10.1 COUNT ON CHANGE

We have already devoted a section above to watching out for change. This includes political, tax, economic as well as changes in management of mutual funds you own, style of investing of those funds and any individual companies you may own. Most of this you will be keeping track of in general just in daily living. But as you do your annual or semi annual or quarterly review of your investments keep the potential for change in mind always.

Always remember that today's darling can be tomorrow's dog. For my money, and probably yours, better the tortoise than the hare! That does not mean a portion of your portfolio should not be devoted to potential home run stocks or funds. But those have to be limited and carefully chosen – and weeded out if conditions change.

Knowing the difference between a major and a minor change is equally important in investing. Marty Zweig in his ads for his market services notes that if you are right on the major direction of interest rates and market activity you will prosper. He is right. The problem is that it is difficult at times to know what that trend is and we are constantly trying to guess the direction of the next move in interest rates and the markets.

But for the busy professional this is best left to those who are professional investors and that is why picking solid mutual funds and doing a minimal amount of timing, mostly by reallocating your portfolios twice a year and evaluating your performance vs a major index once a year will give you the best chance of success.

10.2 SEEDING, WEEDING AND SUCCEEDING

Once you have made a commitment to the markets you need to practice patience. Seldom will the market move straight up the day after you invest. Often the market will move down or move lazily up and down. Months may pass before you see real progress or in some cases years.

While you are waiting you should continue to monitor your progress and with time you have available looking for opportunities. No investment program is fixed in stone as the failure of the nifty fifty of the 1960's showed. To achieve your objectives and earn a reasonable return on the money you have set aside you have to work at developing and improving your investment plan. As the Barron's pamphlet mentioned earlier suggests once a year consider weeding out the weakest of your mutual funds and stocks. It is tempting to develop a buy and hold position and while you should not be jumping in and out of investments neither should you marry your investments. And letting go of a long time winner when its chances for future gain decline or winnowing out a loser rather than holding on hoping it will return to where you invested are both examples of where your intellect has to overcome your natural emotions. Or if you have an investment that has been down and returns to your purchase price you may be tempted to sell when it is exactly the right time to hold on as it may now be moving the direction you wanted.

Always keep in mind that change will always occur. Like watching the ocean creating waves you will know that from the placid water pressures will create a new swell and that once the wave has been created it will continue until it laps the shore. The skill you must develop is to anticipate waves, catch them as they develop and ride them to their conclusion but not when they break against the shore! If you can develop these skills you will ultimately be successful.

10.3 NEVER EAT YOUR SEED CORN

In the early part of this book we used the example of a retired couple with investment funds at their trust department and showed how they were inadvertently eating into their capital while thinking they were living off their income.

This is something that we must all guard against. There may be times in our investment lives when we need to use the capital of our investments for emergencies or temporary living expenses. And if we were investing for a particular purpose and have achieved our goal then of course that is the time to use the investment and achieve your goal. Unlike Midas we are not hoarding our investments just to sit and watch them grow. But if we are to achieve the level of having independent means then we must resist the temptation of excessive current consumption. I say excessive because again, unlike Midas, it does us little good to hoard our money and never use it for enjoyment of life. It is excessive consumption we have to avoid.

We have to always be on guard against eating our seed corn. For example, you might catch a wonderful up wave in the market that increases your investment fund by 100% in a single year. You might be tempted to think "Wow, I really caught that one!" Now since I only hoped to make 25% I can use that other 75% (after paying tax) for some current fun. Wrong! This is sometimes referred to as the "wealth effect" – a feeling of euphoria resulting from a substantial gain in the markets which tempts you to spend some of that money for current consumption. That is what Ben Bernanke is trying to achieve with low interest rates he has imposed on savers since 2008. He wants people taking risks and succeeding and then using that success to buy cars, homes, etc. to stimulate the economy. Good for the Federal Reserve and perhaps the U.S. economy but not necessarily good for your long term future. After that spectacular 100% gain you may well find that in the next year you are down 50% in your investments. Indeed if you follow the suggestions in this book you will make large moves in both directions from time to time. You must use the good years to offset the bad years. Your objective is to make a solid after inflation/after taxes returns over a period of years, some good years and some bad. Not every year but over a period of years. Depending on the level of inflation and taxes you may have to adjust your target. After all what we are after is not a 25%, knowing that is difficult to achieve, but a solid 10% after inflation and after taxes.

It is easy to lose sight of the effect of inflation and taxes and to think we are making money when we are not or think that we are making more money than we really are. So in conclusion let me say that you need to constantly be on guard against diminishing your capital by dipping into it, or to put it more colorfully – don't eat your seed corn.

RESOURCES AND LINKS

Note: Listed below are a few links you may find useful in your investing many of which are mentioned elsewhere in this book. Often these links will change and if so you will need to search for new ones so I have also included the names of particular links for doing a search.

Amazon has available many books including ones on investing some of which are mentioned above. Often older books can be bought through their Marketplace and you may find hardback copies cheaper than paperback. http:// www.amazon.com

American Association of Individual Investors. http:// www.aaii.com

Bloomberg. Also has a good Apple App for free on which you can put your various portfolios and see them updated with totals through the day. Their quotes are, however, delayed 20 minutes. Their news seems to be more up to date than other sources. http://www.bloomberg.com

Bureau of Labor Statistics has an excellent inflation calculator that is easy to use and mentioned several times in this book. It can be found at: http://www.bls.gov/data/inflation_calculator.htm

CEFA is the closed end fund website and you can create a portfolio and view it in ascending or descending order with various screens such as year to date NAV, year to date market value, discounts, etc. Also has useful information on each of the funds. http:// www.cefa.com

CNBC has real time quotes available. A very good Apple App is free. Like Bloomberg you can create one or more portfolios but will not give you daily totals. Will, however, give quotes real time. Also have good sources for pre market futures, commodity prices, bond prices etc. http:// www. cnbc.com

ECRI has useful website I review once a week. Much of it is free and it is too expensive for other than professionals to buy their services. http://www.businesscycle.com/

Federal Reserve website has updates and speeches as well as economic data available at: http://federalreserve.gov/

Ken Fisher who writes for Forbes and manages very large funds has a website that has articles I find useful. http://www.marketminder.com/

Marketwatch from the Wall Street Journal is often a useful source and can be found at: http://www.marketwatch.com/

Morningstar has good sources of information. http:// www. morningstar.com

Savings Bond Calculator is available at: http://www.treasurydirect.gov/BC/SBCPrice

Validea is a useful site for comparison of various portfolio strategies (AAII also does this with their screens free for its members) and the SP500. http:// www.validea.com

Yahoo has excellent news and up to date real time quotes at http:// www.yahoo.com You can create and book mark pages of stock quotes by inserting a comma between quotes. There must be a limit but I have some pages with 50 quotes and works well. However, oddly I have found that sometimes it will give wrong quotes often days or weeks back. So be careful if using and see quote that seems odd. It is a good way to keep up on news on your securities. You can do this for stocks, mutual funds etc. This differs from their portfolio page. To set this up for stocks of interest go to quote and enter your quotes separated by a comma and then save as bookmark. You can then pull up and update for current quotes and news. For closed end funds you can usually insert an "X" before and after a quote to get the NAV end of day e.g., XJRSX will give you the NAV for Nuveen Realty Fund where JRS will give you market quote. They also have excellent charting including interactive charting and a variety of technical tools for those interested. I keep a base chart of the SP500 with candlestick charting, 20 day moving average, 200 day moving average, Bollinger bands, parabolics, MACD, Fast and Slow Stochastics and Money Flow. I keep a separate chart with similar items I can use for individual stocks. Also I keep a chart using line only to compare various stocks in portfolios although you are limited to 5 items at a time. They have an Apple App but it is not as good as their main website. www.finance.yahoo.com

YOUR INDIVIDUAL INVESTMENT PLAN

The items below may help you to organize and think about your investment plan

List Your Objectives For Your Investments:

Do You Have:

1. A Roth IRA? Do you qualify for one?

2. One or more tax deferred accounts such as Traditional IRA, 401(k)?

   A. If you have left an employer have you left your tax deferred account with them? Have you rolled it over to a self directed brokerage or mutual fund account? If not, should you consider doing so?

   B. Have you considered a self directed IRA account?

   C. Have you considered conversion to a Roth IRA to extent possible? Does it make sense for you?

   D. Are the beneficiaries of your accounts up to date? Are any of these held in a TOD or POD account and if so are those designations up to date?

Who do you use to advise you on investments? Do you have a full service broker? A discount broker? A deep discount broker? Do you understand the fees charged such as inactivity fee, annual fee on IRA, etc.

What investments do you have in the following accounts:

Roth IRA:

Traditional IRA:

Other tax deferred account(s) such as 401(k):

Taxable investment accounts:

What steps can you take to improve your investments in these accounts?

Do you have a plan for review and rebalancing your accounts? If so describe here date and manner you plan to review and rebalance

Miscellaneous Items Regarding Your Investments:

At least once a year review the items above and assure yourself that you are doing all you can to achieve the best investment results consistent with your risk comfort level and your objectives for your investments. Add here any items not covered above.